Bandits
Over
Baghdad

Personal Stories of
Flying the F-117 Over Iraq

 Warren E. Thompson

Midland Publishing

ISBN 1 85780 113 X

This edition published by Midland Publishing
24 The Hollow, Earl Shilton
Leicester, LE9 7NA, England
Tel: 01455 847 815   Fax: 01455 841 805
E-mail: midlandbooks@compuserve.com

Midland Publishing is an imprint of
Ian Allan Publishing Ltd.

First published in the United States of America by
Specialty Press Publishers & Wholesalers Inc.
11605 Kost Dam Road, North Branch, MN 55056
Tel: 651-583-3239   Fax: 651-583-2023
Toll free telephone: 800-895-4585

UK and European distribution by
Midland Counties Publications
Unit 3, Maizefield, Hinckley Fields
Hinckley, Leicester, LE10 1YF, Great Britain
Telephone: 01455 233 747   Fax: 01455 233 737
E-mail: midlandbooks@compuserve.com

Printed in the United States of America

Bandits Over Baghdad

Table of Contents

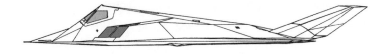

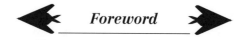

Foreword

Were We Lucky or Good? I Suggest Both.

For those of us who were lucky enough to be part of the F-117 program, especially in the early years, the unprecedented achievements in Desert Storm validated that Stealth technology was a major success and would impact future designs. The performance of the weapons system as well as the military and civilian personnel who supported it, maintained it, and flew it, made their mark in the history of airpower. For almost two decades I've had the opportunity to engage in many memorable events and conversations based on the capabilities, limitations, and accomplishments of the once secret F-117 Nighthawk. These experiences produced some of the real highs (and a few lows) in my personal and professional life.

Most events I recall had something to do with my challenging, rewarding, but limited role in not only the initial deployment, but also the first sustained combat employment of a very capable weapons system. The F-117 has always garnished a great deal of attention, even before its public unveiling in November 1988. However, it's important to note that the Nighthawk has sustained many more "hits" from skeptics and others who were touting their own agenda than it ever has from enemy air defenses!

Recently, I was honored when Warren Thompson asked me to write the foreword to this book. Ironically, at the very moment he called, I was reading an article from the July 5, 1999 *Newsweek*, which was questioning not only the capabilities of the "iron horse" of stealth, but also the Air Force's investment in stealth technology in the B-2 and F-22. It seems that the recent downing of a Nighthawk in Operation Allied Force and combat damage to another had motivated the wolves to cry once again and question our investment in an "imperfect" technology. While I've been reluctant to say much about the F-117 in print or to speak much of my personal experiences, the timing of Warren's call convinced me that fate was calling and I agreed to help him introduce his stories of the Bandits Over Baghdad.

I'd been out of the F-117 business for over seven years when I wrote this. My Nighthawk experience began in early 1981 when I joined the original F-117 unit, the 4450th Tactical Group. On October 15, 1982 under the superb instruction of Major Bill Able, a member of the Combined Test Force, I flew the aircraft for the first time. I became "Bandit #150," the first operational pilot. I left the unit in 1985 for the National War College.

In August 1990, I assumed command of the 37th Tactical Fighter Wing after a whirlwind of assignments that took me to the Pentagon, Red Flag, the 57th Fighter Weapons Wing, and the TAC staff. I took command of the unit only hours before it was tasked to deploy to Desert Shield/Desert Storm. On July 8, 1992, soon after the last F-117 departed Tonopah Test Range, Nevada, the 37th Fighter Wing inactivated. It was the end of an era and the beginning of another as the aircraft were reassigned to the 49th Fighter Wing at Holloman AFB, NM. I cannot speak for the F-117's activities beyond that point since I've had little contact with those in uniform or industry since that time. What I can tell you is that since our return from Desert Storm, the Nighthawk community was overwhelmed with people who claimed to be the father of the F-117. I'm grateful to all of them and for the role they played in creating a very capable weapons system.

While there are some people who have genuinely earned that distinction, I anticipate that the author's purpose is to focus on the courage, commitment, and competence of the many people who worked so diligently to carve a special place in aviation history for the F-117. In Operation Desert Storm, the world quickly learned the value of stealth technology combined with precision guided munitions as they observed the unprecedented results of Team Stealth!

The maintenance, logistics, and operational statistics of the F-117 (and every other weapons system) have been analyzed in every detail by a variety of military and other "expert" agencies. However, no objective analysis can ever measure the personal and professional sacrifices so many men and women made to field this revolutionary technology within a relatively short period of time. While their task was momentous and often an uncharted course, the pioneers of the F-117 program were determined and unrelenting in their efforts to field a revolutionary technology that could have enormous implications for the world!

"Perceptions can be more important than reality" is a phrase and concept well known to politicians. They often do a good job of selling a program to the public when they really may have a totally different agenda. Occasionally, the military deals in deception as a means of secrecy, not only for potential adversaries but also the American public. So it was in the early years of the F-117, when the unit set out to create the perception that it was an A-7 unit dedicated to avionics testing. To pull that off

The 37th Fighter Wing commander throughout both Desert Shield and Desert Storm was Colonel Alton Whitley, shown here in front of an F-117 Nighthawk. Under his leadership, the Wing achieved a record that was almost unimaginable when the war began. He retired from the USAF in 1992 with almost 575 hours in the Stealth fighter. His total number of flying hours during his career came to 5447. He assumed command of the 37th just three days before the first F-117 squadron deployed over to Saudi Arabia during the first week of Desert Shield. (Eric Schulzinger / Lockheed Martin Skunk Works)

while simultaneously fielding a remarkably new weapons system did not come easy. It required tremendous dedication, personal sacrifice, and a level of effort.

However, despite all the great things that came from the F-117 program, there will always be critics with special interests who want to create the perception that stealth technology doesn't work. They want you to believe that it was a bad investment and that somehow it has all been a scam of the American public. Based on my personal experiences, nothing could be any farther from the truth!

No technology is perfect or enduring. We live in a cat and mouse world with rapidly changing technology, strokes and counter strokes, enemies who learn from their mistakes, and potential enemies who steal our technology at every opportunity. What these actual and potential adversaries will find hardest to duplicate will not be the technology, but the dedication and efforts of the men and women of the Nighthawk community who lived up to General Bill Creech's challenge to "Make It Happen," "Make It Better," and "Make It Last."

I want to thank Warren Thompson for the opportunity to introduce his gallant effort to capture the spirit of the men and women who made Team Stealth such a resounding success. Perhaps you'll better appreciate what it was like to live on the edge of new technology, to live a day schedule with your family in Las Vegas on the weekends and a night schedule the rest of the week within the dark confines of the Nellis Range Complex. Following the unprecedented success of the F-117 in Desert Storm, many suggested that airpower will never be the same. All of us who played a role in that success were lucky to be part of something that turned out to be so good!

Alton C. Whitley Jr., Colonel, USAF (Retired)
"Bandit #150"
Commander of 37th Fighter Wing / Desert Storm
22 July 1999

Once the Black Jet went public, increased demand for photographs was instantaneous. The Lockheed Skunk Works was on the cutting edge of this, and some of the most impressive pictures of the F-117 were taken by them at this time. This elevated frontal shot shows the unique lines of the aircraft. It is easy to see how it was able to deflect unfriendly radar in various directions, making it almost invisible to the enemy. It gives off a radar signature equal to that of a small bird, making it impossible to track and lock-on with radar. (Denny Lombard and Eric Schulzinger / Lockheed Martin Skunk Works)

A Word From the Author

In the late 1970s, the spectacular science fiction movie *Star Wars* was released. It captured the imagination of every person who watched it. It represented a futuristic universe that we all knew would never come in our lifetime. However, while none of our military aircraft fly at the speed of light, one of them has already emulated the persona of that movie. If we could have stepped into the 1990s from the year 1977 and seen a picture of the F-117 Nighthawk, we would have believed that maybe Darth Vader had prevailed. This futuristic airframe with its ominous black finish projects an image of exactly what it represents: an invisible night stalker that is capable of hitting any target, anywhere, with absolute precision.

This concept wasn't conceived right before the Gulf War. It was a long time in the planning stages and even longer reaching maturity in its operational mode. The F-117 is living proof that "necessity is the mother of invention." The Vietnam War created an environment that was almost impossible for a conventional aircraft to survive. The sophisticated SAMs and Triple-A played havoc with the F-4 Phantoms and the F-105 Thunderchiefs as they were the deep penetrators tasked with carrying out the bombing missions in Route Package VI which covered Hanoi and Haiphong Harbor. The B-52s were also under heavy pressure from the SAMs.

After the Vietnam war came to an end, the technology on these Soviet-made weapons continued to improve. Not only that, they became readily available to Third World countries. Iraq was probably the biggest customer that Russia had for these weapons, with maybe the exception of the Warsaw Pact countries. Every high-value military asset that Iraq possessed was well defended by state-of-the-art air defenses.

The American military leaders had observed the Iran/Iraq war from a distance. Any serious problems with either of these countries seemed too far fetched to worry about. All of this changed at 2 A.M. Baghdad time on 2 August 1990. Iraq's armed forces crossed over into Kuwait and began an invasion of that country. Unknown to anyone at this time, the F-117 would be the designated executioner that would cut off the head of the Iraqi War Machine. Hidden behind layer after layer of protection, the Iraqi Communication Centers were ready to coordinate the third biggest army in the world in repelling any and all aggressors. Most of the nerve centers were located in and around Baghdad. The loss rate would have been horrendous if conventional aircraft had been required to take out these targets. Enter the Nighthawk!

The following pages will give some insight to a high-tech war as seen through the eyes of the pilots who flew the black jets into the heart of Baghdad. Through a combination of technology, precision-guided bombs, mission planning, and rigid self-discipline, they wrecked all of Iraq's high-value assets and came back home without a scratch. This is the story of Team Stealth at war against the largest military machine in the Middle East. The author shares stories told by the leaders, pilots, and mission planners who worked together to compile a record unheard of in any prior war.

The vast majority of this book is comprised of verbatim accounts from the pilots who flew the F-117 out of the Tonopah Test Range and in the Gulf War. In many cases, the same missions or incidents are discussed by several pilots. This provides the reader with several different angles and points of view, giving a detailed, three-dimensional slant. This story belongs to all of the men and women who were associated, in any way, with stealth operations during the Gulf War. Therefore, it must be told in their own words!

Warren E. Thompson

Chapter One

The Tonopah Days

N o story on the F-117 would be complete without mentioning the formative years, when the aircraft was just becoming operational. It was during this period that the deadly effective tactics for the Nighthawk were being formulated and perfected. It was a time when the entire project was hidden away in a "black hole" known as the Tonopah Test Range Airfield, located in a desolate desert region 140 miles northwest of Las Vegas, Nevada. Actually, what went on there, day-to-day, is not well known. The personnel involved in the early Stealth program were sworn to secrecy and that mind fix still survives today, in early 2000.

In 1979, while the aircraft was still in its infancy, the first official organization to utilize it , operationally, was the 4450th Tactical Group. All personnel, officers and enlisted, were carefully select-ed to participate in this new program. This same airfield had existed for many years, but it was, by no means, capable of han-dling a major project such as this one.

The first flight of the F-117 was in June 1981. With the Lockheed Skunk Works cranking up into full production right after that, the green light was given to begin expanding the base at Tonopah. This was begun in early 1982 and finished in almost record time. The entire project was on a tight schedule and with the new fighter becoming operational in the Fall of 1983, the work had to be far enough along to begin receiving the F-117s as they were accepted by the Air Force.

Becoming operational with the Nighthawk would put a hardship on the family life of everyone involved in the program. It was like

During the Tonopah days, after the public had been informed of the existence of this ominous looking Stealth fighter, there were numerous photo opportunities that Lockheed Martin participated in. The 2,000-pound bomb shown here was the GBU-10, one of the special weapons carried by the F-117. It proved to be extremely effective against bridges and smaller targets that did not require the deep penetration of the GBU-27. (USAF via the Dennis R. Jenkins Collection)

nothing that had been experienced before, short of war. The pilots and enlisted personnel would leave their homes and families early Monday mornings and return late each Friday. They would be flown up to Tonopah where they were involved in a nighttime only training operation that demanded long hours. When they returned to their families each weekend, they could not and would not discuss anything that had occupied their time during the week. Early on, the word was that they were part of a special weapons test involving the A-7. This explanation was widely accepted and remained intact until the Air Force decided to reveal the secret to the American public. In November 1988, an announcement was made to the press that the F-117A Stealth fighter did, indeed, exist. This caused a frenzy of news coverage and without a doubt, it probably caused some grave concerns within the walls of the Kremlin.

For several years, the Stealth had been flown only at night and within the confines of the vast range over Nevada. The experience level and tactics had been improved only to a certain degree as there had been too many restrictions regarding when and where the aircraft could operate. It was the need to expand operations to a higher degree that brought down the cloak of secrecy. This meant that the F-117 could not only fly during the day, but now it could become integrated into a viable strike package with other aircraft types. These multi-force training exercises were constantly being tried and tested at Red Flag.

Recovering at its base at Tonopah, this F-117 returns from an orientation flight in the area during the daylight hours. New Stealth pilots spend a lot of time flying in the general area of the base to get the feel of how the aircraft handles, before they start working into the operational phase of flying the night missions and gaining the experience necessary to take the machine into a hostile environment. Before they solo in the aircraft, they spend countless hours of "flight time" in the simulator. (Lockheed Martin Skunk Works)

Now, for the first time, the real potential of the Stealth could reach maturity and this would eventually be manifested in Desert Storm.

The 4450th Tactical Group achieved operational status in October 1983, long before the war in the Desert began. The training, at night, went on week after week. A large number of the Air Force pilots who were in the early Stealth operations when the tactics manual was being written, had moved on to other programs or had exited the military, by the time Desert Shield rolled around. A significant percentage of the pilots who saw combat in Grenada and the Gulf, had come into the program in the late 1980s. Some had as few as 50 hours in the jet.

A lone Stealth eases out of its protected hangar for another mission over the Tonopah range. Note the double row of security fences that protect the hangars and aircraft. This was taken after the F-117 had forfeited its top-secret status to the world's media, allowing the aircraft to begin extensive daytime flights. This gave the pilots more cockpit time, even though their serious training missions were always at night. (Lockheed Martin Skunk Works)

In October 1989, the 4450th TG was redesignated as the 37th Tactical Fighter Wing. The lineage of the 37th went all the way back to pre-World War II days. During the Cold War years, the unit had flown both the F-100 and the F-4. In the course of only one year, the 37th would be vaulted into the history books with an unbelievable success rate against heavily defended targets, that had never been heard of before.

The regimen and secrecy that surrounded the Black Operations at Tonopah were second to none within the U.S. military. Major Dale "Sledge" Hanner (Bandit #239) relates a few details about those formative days north of Las Vegas. "To get to our secluded area, you had to cross a lot of desert and then pass through two

This aerial view of the Tonopah facilities was taken after the massive expansion program had been completed. Note the long rows of hangars in the center of the photo which housed the entire F-117 inventory. Access to the hangar area was protected by a double row of fences. The security at Tonopah was second to none, even after the F-117 had come into public view. The flying distance over to Nellis AFB was 140 miles. (Lockheed Martin Skunk Works)

Surrounded by a world of darkness, this Stealth pilot has complete situational awareness of everything around him, as he closes in on his unsuspecting target. Note the all-important target images that are positioned on his right leg. Using this distinct imaging, he can line up the crosshairs on the target and the precision ordnance can be delivered through a doorway or down a ventilation shaft. This new brand of warfare has probably stopped more potential adversaries than anyone will ever know. (Lockheed Martin Skunk Works)

guarded Entry Control Points, then a double-fenced area with a palm-reader, then get past the cipher lock on the squadron door and into the safe sitting inside another, larger walk-in safe. Aircraft hangar doors were never opened until 30 minutes after sunset. Taxiing could be a little risky, because you were not allowed to use the taxi light if it would shine on another 'asset.' Often this meant pulling into the arming area taxiing in total darkness (except for the blue taxiway edge lighting). If a truck happened to get in your way, you just hit it! It never happened, but it was always a relief to get airborne, where the aircraft were supposed to be!

"All of the aircraft had to be down by 0330 hours (3:30 A.M.), so that all signs of operations and activity could be shut down and packed away before sunrise. The pressure of flying under this cloak of secrecy during the week and being a husband/father compressed into a short weekend, left us dirt-tired all the time. It was determined that going to bed before you saw the sun beginning to rise helped maintain some semblance of circadian rhythm, and thus became a requirement. This, along with very seriously stressing adequate crew rest (16 hours minimum during the summer, when the takeoffs were latest) did indeed improve safety."

The first "public viewing" of the Stealth at Nellis AFB was one of the top news stories of the day. Unknown at this time was the fact that four months after this picture was taken, these aircraft would be loaded with bombs and ready to fly combat missions on a moment's notice, several thousand miles away. One year later, the F-117 would have rewritten many of the records that had been established in past wars, proving to be the most lethal weapon in the U.S. arsenal. (Skunk Works)

During their nightly training missions, the planners and pilots were not content to go after the more obvious targets within their limited Nevada realm, but they singled out some of the smallest targets that could be found. These "friendly" Stealth missions were planned, briefed, and executed just as if they were in a war with everything on the line. It was this mind-set that paid off in a big way when the F-117 went into combat during the Gulf War.

The F-117 gives one the impression that it is a very small aircraft. True, it is a single-seat fighter, but it also carried two jet engines and two 2,000-pound bombs. This picture shows a head-on view and a comparison of size with a large tow vehicle. Compared to the Vietnam era F-105 Thunderchief, it is small, but its capacity to deliver precision-guided bombs with such destructive power makes it a much more effective bomb platform than anything from that period. This was taken at Tonopah prior to the beginning of Desert Shield. (Eric Schulzinger / Lockheed Martin Skunk Works)

From the early days when the "Black Jet" went operational, it had always been accustomed to the best enclosed shelters that were available and rightly so, considering how important it was proven to be to the overall attack force. These new facilities were built specifically for the F-117 at Tonopah and have not housed an entire operational unit since the Stealth pulled out after the Gulf War and moved to Holloman AFB, New Mexico. (Lockheed Martin Skunk Works)

Major Wesley Wyrick (Bandit #330), a 415th Squadron pilot, was one of the first to deploy over to Saudi Arabia during early Desert Shield. He recalls those intense night training missions in which each of the Stealth pilots honed their skills. "The training routes we flew had a wide variation, but in general, were much tougher than combat targets. The mission planners would target houses, shopping center type complexes, government buildings plus the standard range targets (aircraft hulks in revetments), but the favorite was the plastic 'Tough Sheds.' This was a brand name for small utility sheds that were sold in Nevada and they were usually about 4' x 6'. Most were placed in backyards under a tree. The 'Tough Sheds' were low IR gradient targets 'delta T' (did not show well since the temperature difference was small from its surroundings).

A narrow field of frontal visibility is all the pilot needs. The aircraft will fly a pre-designed route that has been fed into the onboard computer. Complete 360-degree vision is unnecessary in an aircraft that has been designed for night operation only. The daytime dogfighting has been left up to the F-15 Eagle and a few other types, but the subsonic speed of the F-117 would make it a sitting duck during the day. (Eric Schulzinger / Lockheed Martin Skunk Works)

On 21 April 1990, two F-117s flew from Tonopah down to Nellis AFB for the sole purpose of letting the public view the aircraft close up. A tremendous crowd was present to witness this top-secret futuristic fighter. Security was tight and the media was allowed to take pictures closer than they had ever been before. The viewing was followed by a press conference held in the auditorium in which the media was allowed to interview and question the Stealth pilots and maintenance person-nel. Within hours, the pictures and news releases had made it to all cor-ners of world. (Buck Taylor)

"We regularly targeted the 4450th Group commander's house at Nellis! The target sets included stuff in Sacramento (Government buildings and industry) all the way back to Tahoe (small houses in the trees) and on to every type of electrical junction and petro-leum stores. On one Turkey Shoot night, I remember a telephone booth was a target. Just to make things more interesting, some of the town targets were 'late show,'* since we were routed over

---

* "Late Show" refers to a target that is difficult to line up because it doesn't come into view until just seconds before a bomb is to be dropped. For example, a Stealth is over a mountainous area and the target is immediately on the other side of one of the ridges, but no visual sight can be made on the target until the Stealth is over the top of it. This allows the pilot only seconds to locate and lock on before time to drop the ordnance.

When the existence of the Stealth was revealed in 1988, it freed up the F-117 to begin flying during the day. This photo was taken long before Desert Shield started, somewhere over the desert in Nevada. The aircraft's subsonic speed would have made it an easy target for enemy fighters if it had been seen. Fortunately, this never happened and later, during the war, it proved that under cover of darkness, it was truly invisible. (Eric Schulzinger / Lockheed Martin Skunk Works)

a mountain ridge and the target was in a valley. This would further compress the acquisition and tracking time. We didn't have much time to visually acquire and hit the target. I credit a good portion of the success we had in the war to the excellent training we got every night, flying out of Tonopah."

Every pilot assigned to the two front-line squadrons of Stealth Fighters (415th and 416th) would attest to the wide variety of practice targets that they went up against. Even the pilots who were in the 417th Training Squadron were subjected to this regimen. Major Jon Boyd, a veteran of numerous F-117 combat missions over Iraq reflects on some of the tougher "targets" that he went after, prior to his deployment to the middle East.

"You could pick just about anything as long as it broke out in the IRADS. A few memorable ones were tombstones in a cemetery in some small towns in Nevada, a guy's new hot tub in a backyard in Las Vegas, and the favorite 'Tuff Shed' which could have been in any backyard from the Vegas area all the way over to Sacramento, California. We would also 'sport bomb' from a fairly high altitude with BDUs out on the range. Our accuracy was exceptionally good! About the time that Iraq invaded Kuwait, I had accumulated almost 280 hours in the Stealth, all of which was from flying the tough night practice missions."

From the time the F-117 became operational and on through Desert Shield and Storm, it had always operated in an environment that it was accustomed to and its hangar facilities were first rate! These new hangars were especially built, at Tonopah, for the new Stealth aircraft. When they arrived at Khamis Mushait in August 1990, they were quartered in new hardened-aircraft shelters that had been built for the F-15s of the Saudi Air Force. All aspects of servicing these planes could easily be done within the confines of the shelters. (Lockheed Martin Skunk Works)

While the collective "hit list" compiled from the pilot's memory banks was impressive, there was one regular target that would have mustered far more attention from the public had it been brought to light. Several pilots have stated that they targeted second base at a major baseball stadium on a regular basis. At this stage of their training, they could easily have delivered a precision hit on that small a target! In all reality, there was no structure completely safe, within the borders of the United States, after dark. The nighttime over friendly skies belonged to the Black Jet and there was nothing in the arsenal of any country, including the USA, that could stop it.

This angle shows the unique, futuristic-looking profile of the F-117. The ominous Nighthawk was capable of delivering precision bombs during the hours of darkness with such accuracy, that there were no known targets, in Iraq, that would be considered safe. This photo shows how the two 2,000-pound smart bombs are loaded into the bomb bays of the aircraft. This was taken at Tonopah before the 37th Fighter Wing began deploying to Saudi Arabia. (Lockheed Martin Skunk Works)

With the 415th Squadron already in place at Khamis Mushait, the 416th Squadron was working overtime back at Tonopah. Intel sent to the 416th from the 415th helped planners develop effective tactics against potential targets. Fortunately, both squadrons had the time to test and discard plans that would not work. This picture was taken at Tonopah in 1990. (Eric Schulzinger / Lockheed Martin Skunk Works)

Originally, Stealth pilots were shaped and trained in an organization that would use the aircraft for one- and two-ship precision strikes such as was its involvement in Panama. This was the first time that the F-117 had been used in a hostile situation. The single-ship strategy evolved into a much more sophisticated regimen, one in which multiple aircraft would carry out simultaneous attacks. This was greatly enhanced by the fact that the program had finally come out of the "black" and public knowledge of the aircraft's existence would allow the Stealth to become even more effective.

At this point in time, the F-117 was poised to move great distances out of its Tonopah base and strike targets all over the

This KC-135 is refueling an F-117 at dusk over the Nevada desert prior to Desert Storm. Most of the hookups on practice missions between the tankers and the Nighthawks were done in total darkness just as they would be at the Iraqi border later on. Some of the combat missions flown during the war were very lengthy. The standard missions in and around Baghdad were the same distance as flying from a base in southeast Texas all the way up into Maine and returning. On many missions flown up to the Turkish border, the tankers had to fly deep into Iraq to make sure the F-117 had enough fuel to get back out. (Lockheed Martin Skunk Works)

United States. Captain Mark Renelt (Bandit #264) recalls a major event that opened the doors for the development of new tactics.

"Our first trip east of the Mississippi River was an 8+ hour round-trip to the Eglin AFB Ranges for a well-planned precision strike, all under the cover of darkness. If memory serves me correctly, I believe there were six F-117s and two tankers involved in the mission. The strike configuration would be two groups of three aircraft each. Planning for the mission was most interesting because most agencies were not used to dealing with us. We were just out of the 'black world.' Also, Eglin didn't have a lot of target pictures that we could use. We began the mission with a tanker pickup. I believe we designed the pickup to insure minimum exposure to prying eyes/radar. The tanker would overfly the field and the Stealth would take off to be joined up by the time we left the airport traffic area. The only thing Air Traffic Control (ATC) would see was a formation of tankers. After we joined, we climbed out of the restricted areas where the tankers gave me my first opportunity to do a lost-wingman procedure, when they flew through the darkest cloud I have ever been in!

It would be difficult to distinguish whether a picture had been taken in Saudi Arabia or Nevada, unless you knew the date and location of the picture. These two F-117s rest on the ramp at Tonopah in early 1990. The elevations above sea level between Tonopah and Khamis were very similar, so there were no major changes in terrain when the Stealth squadrons deployed, thus they were right at home with the lay-of-the-land during Shield and Storm. (Denny Lombard / Lockheed Martin Skunk Works)

"The flight to Eglin was rather uneventful. The tankers let us off south of the Eglin ranges which put us out over the Gulf of Mexico. From this position, we marshaled for our attack runs on a simulated enemy airfield. Following the strikes, we exited the target areas to the east and then south to rejoin with the tankers. After that was accomplished, we faced the long flight back to Nevada."

Once the Stealth pilots began ranging out great distances, they did not know it at the time, but they were conditioning themselves for a war that was not too far in the future: Desert Storm. With the F-117's new freedom to range out to distant targets, a new problem cropped up: pilot fatigue. With a small cramped cockpit, it was impossible to stand up or get any exercise. Physical conditioning took some of the edge off as did numerous lengthy missions, but it was next to impossible to counter the effects on the pilots of a seven- or eight-hour mission.

As the scope of their nocturnal operations expanded, other problems appeared. One of these involved the all-important tape machine that was built into the F-117. It provided the sole documentation of what was being accomplished on these practice missions and it measured the success and accuracy of "bomb" deliveries. Captain Renelt said, "In addition to some other things, we found that our tape machines destroyed our tapes after many hours of standby. After that first long mission to the Eglin area, they were modified so that we could turn them off completely and be able to record our hits later. This was absolutely essential in finding out how well we were doing."

This fact was reinforced by Major Hanner's comments regarding what was done to correct the problem. The fix on this had to be immediate because of the new long-range missions being flown by the F-117 pilots. "It turned out that, unbeknownst to anyone, the Video Tape Recorder (VTR), when selected to 'off' by the pilot, actually went to 'standby,' meaning the tape stayed threaded in the recorder. This left the head spinning on the tape and it eventually wore it out. No one realized this until we flew an eight-hour mission and most of the tapes stopped recording! This led to a modification which changed the 'off' position to actually being 'off.' The result being that although it took a couple of extra seconds after selecting 'on' for the tape to start recording (while it spooled up), thus the tapes were working at the end of a long mission."

The namesake of the F-117 was the ominous "Nighthawk." It was the all-seeing, nocturnal predator that could swoop down on the darkest night and kill even the smallest of its prey. Its traits fit the Stealth fighter perfectly. (Lockheed Martin Skunk Works)

While the pilots and their Nighthawks grabbed the headlines, it was the professional skills and attitude of the support personnel that kept the precision-bombing Stealth aircraft over the heavily defended targets every night of the war. This photo was taken at Tonopah prior to the hostilities. These specialists are fine tuning one of the General Electric F-404 turbofan engines that drive the F-117. (Lockheed Martin Skunk Works)

Chapter Two

Operation Desert Shield

The year 1990 proved to be monumental in the history of the Lockheed "Black Jet." On 21 April, the F-117 had its public debut at Nellis AFB, Nevada. It was a world event with members of the media converging from all parts of the globe. Tens of thousands of curious onlookers crowded the ramp at Nellis for a first-hand glimpse. Less than two months later, the 59th and final Stealth fighter was delivered to the USAF's Tactical Air Command (June 1990). All three squadrons were at full complement and the intense training regimen was at full bore. The old saying "All dressed up and no place to go" was not meant for the 37th Fighter Wing because the invasion of Kuwait by the Iraqis on 2 August 1990 was about to catapult them into the world spotlight. As history will attest, they did deliver!!

The 37th was made up of three squadrons which were steeped in tradition dating back to early 1943 during the early stages of World War II. The 415th, 416th, and 417th squadrons had flown the twin engine British-made Beaufighter and Mosquito in the Mediterranean Theatre of Operations. Strangely enough, the squadrons had a specialty in the fledgling art of Night Fighting. They had a phenomenal record in North Africa and Italy. During the final days of the war, they converted over to the deadly P-61 Black Widow. The Luftwaffe felt their sting in the darkness. At war's end, the 415th had eleven confirmed kills, the 416th had five, and the 417th had nine. On top of this impressive total was a staggering 24 enemy aircraft damaged or probables. Now, here it was almost 50 years later, and all three squadrons still maintained a nocturnal mission. But, this time, it was with such deadly precision that the F-117's capabilities could never have even been dreamed of during the 1940s. Now, the task was to destroy high-value enemy assets that were protected ten times better than any target had been in World War II.

From 1979 through early 1990, the Iraq military machine had developed into a world-class power that was ranked in the top five. The entire country was an armed camp that had fought a long war with its neighbor, Iran, and still increased in power as it went along. At no time did Iran bleed any military strength off of Saddam Hussein's total force. During this time, the Iraqi gov-

Colonel Al Whitley, Wing C.O. on the left and 416th Fighter Squadron C.O., Lt.Colonel Greg Gonyea relax after the long flight from Tonopah to Langley AFB, Virginia. This was just the first leg on the long flight to Saudi Arabia to join the 415th Squadron at Khamis Mushait. The time was early December 1990, with the Gulf War still about six weeks away. Note the round 416th squadron emblem painted on the right side of Lt. Colonel Gonyea's F-117. (G.T. Gonyea)

ernment had continued to sell huge amounts of petroleum and borrowed large sums of money from fellow Arab countries to finance the Iran/Iraq War. When the dust settled on that war, Iraq found itself deeply in debt to Kuwait. With some futile efforts to get the Kuwaitis to forgive the debt, Hussein decided it would be better to consume the country and therefore there would be no debts to worry about. On 2 August, he did just that. The takeover was so swift that it was feared Saudi Arabia might be next. For some reason or another, the Iraqis hesitated. This allowed the United States and its Allies to get all their forces mustered and ready to stop the aggression.

On Classified orders cut on 13 August 1990 (Travel Order #TJ-013), the 415th Fighter Squadron was ordered to deploy to the Middle East to support an operation that would be known as Desert Shield. This elite F-117 unit would be one of the first Air Force operational squadrons to be ordered into this highly volatile situation. Listed on the orders were 22 pilots along with the squadron operations officer, Lt. Colonel Barry E. Horne and the 415th Squadron commander, Lt. Colonel Ralph W. Getchell. Within hours they were all but prepared to make the move, but it wasn't going to be that easy! The incredible demand for tanker support proved to be a problem. Also, a major air base had to be secured for the Stealth fighters to operate out of and this base had to be as far from harm's way as was possible. While the USAF was willing to commit its most sophisticated aircraft into this potential war, it was going to insure that the personnel and planes were going to be far enough away from the Iraqi border that the threat of missiles and terrorist attacks was minimal! It took a few days to get the base lined up, located at King Khalid Air Base in the extreme southwestern corner of Saudi Arabia. During the war, it would be referred to as Khamis Mushait.

Captain Rob Donaldson (Bandit #321) recalls the days right after the movement orders were cut. "Only our 415th Squadron 'Night Stalkers' was involved in the initial deployment. It was nerve-wracking because we kept getting the 'go — don't go' .... I believe the delays were caused by the fact they were trying to secure a base for us to operate out of. I can remember one time, we were actually walking out the door to go to our aircraft when the flight was cancelled again. These delays were frustrating to all the pilots, but it did give us a few more days with our families."

Within two days of their departure, tensions had grown considerably. This was brought on by a combination of things such as the mounting publicity being given to the crisis by the media and the pilots not knowing exactly when they would launch. To relieve this, some of the pilots had the opportunity to go up in the T-38s and fly some acrobatics over Tonopah. Major George Kelman (Bandit #281) was one of the few who took advantage of this release. He went out and put on a minor air show, over the base, for all of the ground personnel that were interested enough to watch. He stated that he was much more relaxed when he landed. Actually there was very little that any of the pilots could do to relieve the type of pressure that they were under; knowing they were going to war but not knowing when, and the fact that their families were only a short distance away but there was nothing they could do about it.

Perhaps, the person caught in the most difficult position was the new 37th Wing Commander, Colonel Alton Whitley. He had been associated with the program during its early stages before he departed in 1985 for other assignments. Now, he had been given the responsibility of the only Stealth Wing in the Air Force and all of this came about the time that Iraq invaded Kuwait. The official Change of Command ceremony took place on 16 August 1990, when Wing Commander Colonel Tony Tolin turned the command flag of the 37th over to Colonel Whitley. Two days later, Whitley was on a C-5 Galaxy bound for the Stealth's new base in Saudi Arabia.

The flow of events for the first mass movement of the F-117 into a hostile environment went as follows: The 415th Fighter Squadron launched 22 fighters from Tonopah for Langley AFB Virginia, which would be the only "rest stop" on the long flight over. Colonel Whitley and the 415th Squadron commander, Lt.

One of the best "shooters" to come out of Desert Storm is shown here riding in the back of a "Humvee" along the forward positions during the Gulf War. T/Sgt. Rose S. Reynolds of the 2nd Combat Camera Unit took most of the pictures that were officially sanctioned by the USAF, of F-117 Operations at Khamis Mushait. Her outfit was based out of Norton AFB, California at the time. (Combat Camera)

Colonel Ralph Getchell, made the flight over in a C-5 with all of the critical gear that included the mission planning equipment. While in flight, Lt. Colonel Getchell brought Whitley up-to-date on everything that the squadron was capable of doing along with an outline of current tactics. To say that this was a "pressure briefing" would have been an understatement. The 415th's Operations Officer, Lt. Colonel Barry Horne, remained at Langley AFB while his pilots were getting ready for the flight. He went down to Seymour-Johnson AFB to brief all of the tanker crews on the plans. When it came time for the mass launch, Lt. Colonel Horne was positioned in the lead tanker for the crossing.

For the short period that the large number of F-117s had been at Langley, they had created an enormous amount of attention, both from the media and from the area's residents. To see those aircraft parked and ready to defend the freedom of others, must have been an emotional time for those behind the fences. Major Wesley Wyrick vividly recalls that moment. "It was one of the most emotional sights that I have ever seen. As we taxied to park our aircraft on the dead runway at Langley, all of the families and personnel from the base housing area were lined up waving American flags. I will always remember the fence lined with flags and the thumbs up from all of the people positioned shoulder to shoulder along the way." Perhaps this sudden call to arms marked the end of a long drought, dating back to 1950. This time the American people were totally behind the events that were about to unfold!! In the meantime, while all the excitement was going on outside, the focussed Stealth pilots were attending briefings that involved their upcoming transatlantic flight to Saudi Arabia.

Finally, it was "Show Time." All 22 of the aircraft launched from Langley and the weather off the coast of Virginia was lousy. The game plan called for four of the aircraft to act as ready spares in case there were any aborts from the primary 18. At a predetermined point out over the Atlantic, if there was no indication of problems with the main force of fighters, the four spares turned around and flew back to Langley and then on back to Tonopah. The formation spread called for two F-117s assigned to each KC-10 tanker. Major Kelman remembers the flight. "We got airborne and the military controllers weren't much help when we were trying to join up with our tankers out over the water in bad weather! So, I had to cycle back and forth between the tanker and back to my wingman, so I wouldn't lose him. Our six-ship was taking evasive action by going around clouds and still trying to stay as close to the track line as possible. We finally broke out of the bad weather about ten minutes before we would have had to turn around and head back to Langley. That forty minutes of trying to get out of the Langley area and about 200 miles out over the water was the most demanding part of the entire ocean cross-

The tanker of choice, during Desert Storm, was the KC-10 shown here. These oversized fuel "trucks" would position themselves on a predetermined track, waiting for the F-117s to egress out of Iraq. After the long missions into enemy territory, they were always very low on fuel and it was essential for the tankers to be in position when they were needed. The Stealths would usually pick up their tankers after takeoff from Khamis Mushait and would take them all the way to the Saudi / Iraq borders. Normally, there were two of these nocturnal bombers assigned to one KC-10. (Lockheed Martin Skunk Works)

ing to Saudi Arabia! We spent more energy during that brief period than we did on the rest of the long flight!" It should be noted here that all of the 415th aircraft were loaded with two 2000-pound bombs at Tonopah prior to their long flight to the Middle East. They were prepared for the possibility of having to fly combat missions within 24 hours of their arrival at Khamis Mushait.

During the long 15-hour flight over the Atlantic and Mediterranean, the subject of which base they would land at was still undecided. Once they left the bad weather, it proved to be a memorable, but tiring flight. Though the pilots began to tire by

In a rare daylight flight, this F-117 is pictured over a famous Saudi Arabian resort north of the air base at Khamis Mushait. The resort was built at a higher elevation than the base which would put the resort about 9,000 feet above sea level. This flight was probably to check out the fighter after it had undergone maintenance. Located two and a half hours flying time from the Iraqi border, this area was deemed safe from any attack from the air or ground, with the exception of a possible attack coming out of Yemen, which was to the south. (Rob Donaldson)

the time they made landfall over North Africa, all of them commented on the beauty of the terrain. Major Wesley Wyrick (Bandit #330) recalls his impressions of the final leg of the trip. "We cut across Malta, on north of Libya, hitting the northern tip of Egypt and the vast sea of sand. Even as we flew over the Red Sea, none of us were sure where we were going to land, but we continued on in the direction of Khamis Mushait in Saudi Arabia. We could talk to the tankers through the hookup and even they didn't know where we were going to end up! There was no feedback coming from the F-117s that were out in front of us. Finally, we arrived over our destination and there was no radio transmission from the tower at Khamis, so without hesitation, my lead wingman, Major Dan Backus, led us right into the pattern and landed. As we touched down and taxied in, we still had no idea what frequency the tower was on! Some of our support personnel landed about one and a half hours before we did and that was the first time the Saudis knew we were coming!"

Fifteen hours in any cockpit is extremely hard on the body, regardless of one's age or physical conditioning. The fact that the F-117 was a single seat with no room for moving around compounded the situation. Major Kelman relates their arrival at Khamis. "Things were really hopping on the ground! As soon as we landed, we were told to hurriedly taxi into our hardened-aircraft shelters. Our ground crews were ordered to get our planes ready to fly combat within 24 hours. For all we knew, we would be flying missions that night! But this did not happen. We were really beat by the time we arrived at our base. Some of us had to be helped out of the cockpit by the enlisted guys that were around the aircraft. I remember that after we climbed down, somebody handed me a 'near beer.' We had been in the cockpit for about 17 hours and in the air for 15 of those and all we got for it was one 'near beer!!' I guess it could have been worse."

The 415th had found a home at one of the most modern air bases in the world. It was brand new and built for the Saudi Air Force's F-15 Eagles. Perhaps it was too new, because the troops found it tough going, at least for a few days. The water had to be turned on and there was very little food available for several days. The MREs (aka: instant meals) arrived later and even though there wasn't enough of them to go around, the troops made do. Over the next few weeks, just about every member of the 37th who had deployed, suffered a minor loss of weight. Some of the pilots estimated that the average weight loss among their ranks ranged from 10 to 20 pounds. Arrangements were made to bring in more "American" food and after a month or so of hardships, things began to level off. Coca Colas were hard to come by and alcohol was not allowed due to religious customs of the country.

There were two major benefits of being based at Khamis in that it was surrounded by a vast desert terrain supplemented by rugged mountains and its elevation was 6700' above sea level. In other words, it was almost identical to the ranges in Nevada. The similarity was so great that the Saudi air base was nicknamed "Tonopah East." The Stealth pilots would be flying and fighting in very similar surroundings to what they were used to training in for years. Another obvious asset to the base was that it was hunkered down in the extreme southwest corner of Saudi Arabia, which put it out of danger from Iraqi missile attacks. During the first six weeks that the 415th was cocked and ready to shoot, there was very little flying time. This was due to the fact, they were loaded with ordnance and ready to take the war all the way to downtown Baghdad. As the situation calmed down and a clearer picture formed, those in command of Desert Shield realized that the Allied forces were going to be allowed to build up to a comfortable strength and that the diplomats were going to make an effort to solve the standoff without a war. During this period, the F-117 pilots began flying just enough to keep up their proficiency, taking part in training sorties every other night.

However well defended the remote base was, there was still a possibility of an air attack coming up from the nearby Yemeni border. To counter this threat, the Saudi Air Force flew a 24-hour CAP between the base and Yemen in F-15s. One night, a Saudi Eagle pilot was having mechanical trouble with his aircraft and was being led through a violent weather front that had moved into the area. An American fighter pilot was on his wing when the F-15 lost its generators and crashed, killing the pilot. After that, the Saudis decided that it was too dangerous to fly CAPs at night, so they discontinued them. From that time on, they only flew the protective barrier patrols during the day. This put the pressure on a Hawk missile battery that was on base which provided adequate protection against the potential threat that never materialized. The fact that the aircraft were kept secure in their hardened shelters reduced the possibility of any damage from such an attack.

Major Joe Salata takes on fuel from a KC-10 tanker while practicing over the Saudi desert during Desert Shield. During their night operations, there were usually two F-117s assigned to one KC-10. Each would take up station off a designated wing of the tanker en route to the Iraqi border. During the brief war, the weather over Iraq was the worst in years. This required the fighters to position themselves just a few feet off each wing in order to keep the small lights on the tanker's wingtips in sight. By the time they reached the border and were ready to fly their assigned mission, the pilots were exhausted because of the precision flying required in zero weather. (Rose Reynolds)

Every member of the 37th Wing (Deployed) took each day as it came because there was no way to know what would happen the next day. Although there was almost no flying the first few weeks, the base was a beehive of activity. The 415th mission planners immediately received a list of the targets that had been selected for the first night of the war—whenever that was to be. The pilots slept in the hardened shelters at four to a room with a common bathroom. The mission planning cell was located inside these protective enclosures and the planners were totally engrossed in setting up the routes and avoiding the threats for each Stealth that would be sent across the Iraqi border on the first two nights.

Once the sleeping quarters were squared away and the meals began to improve, there was still the problem of boredom, especially on a base where security was at its highest level. Perimeter security was provided by the Colorado Air National Guard which was committed to the task. The threat of terrorist attacks was very real and the Iraqis were bound to have been informed as to where the F-117s were based. For entertainment, there were only two movies, "Pretty Woman" or "Total Recall." Each night the sequence of movies would change; one night "Pretty Woman" was viewed first and then vice versa. It wasn't long before the pilots could mouth the words with the characters in the film. Some of the pilots enjoyed a visit to the McDonnell-Douglas Tech Rep facilities which had an exercise room and pool. Working out and grabbing some sun was probably the best thing for morale, at least until the war started.

Although the terrain was very similar, the F-117 pilots and tacticians worked at a steady pace to make sure they were using the right tactics and planning to take out the long list of targets that they would be given for the first three nights. Major Kelman indicates how the 415th's way of thinking changed somewhat from earlier days at Tonopah. "We immediately set up a training scenario as we decided on our tactics and to work ourselves into those tactics. We were going to do things a little different than we had done them back in the states...more mass attacks. In order to do that, we had to practice them to keep our timing down to zero/zero or as close as we could to that number. Realistically, when we first started, we were anywhere from 15 to 20 seconds on the mass target attacks but by the time our practice sessions were in full swing, we were happy with it as our time was down to within six seconds. That is, we could put as many as twelve aircraft over a single target area and all the bombs would impact within six seconds. It took about six weeks of intense repetition to accomplish this spacing. Keep in mind that all of this was done under the cover of total darkness." It should be noted here that the gap continued to narrow as the war progressed. Some of these missions will be covered later in the book.

The targets that been selected for the first night went through a constant changing process. As the intelligence people gained information and new targets began cropping up, there were new enemy assets being discovered that would have priority over some that had been known about at the outset of Desert Shield. As time would prove, the entire country of Iraq was an arsenal with unlimited storage facilities. Major Kelman speaks rather bluntly about the intelligence the Stealth planners were receiving early on. "In the preparation for the war, during the Desert Shield period, there were a lot of personality conflicts up at the higher levels which caused us, early on, not to receive the best information that we could have. So, we went at it in a roundabout way and got what we needed. We sent messages back to the states on our satellite system to retrieve the necessary data allowing our planners to be effective. As you know, the Stealth team is very dedicated to knowing the latest intelligence down to the 'nth degree! Without that, the stealthiness, in design and route planning, is at a slight disadvantage. The fact that we survived all those missions was a testament to that ability to acquire the intelligence required! A lot of its success had to do with poor or mediocre gunners, but a significant amount had to do with the amount of knowledge obtainable from electronic sources. Our people were able to get what they needed to make us one of the most effective strikers in the Gulf War."

As the days and weeks of Desert Shield laboriously passed by, the intensity of the training missions picked up in tempo. The Saudis opened up a bomb range to the Stealth Wing and this allowed them to practice newer, more effective tactics. It had been closed down for over a year, so it would not have been considered state-of-the-art. Major Kelman became the Range Officer and through his efforts, a significant amount of supplies and equipment were diverted to the range's use. It was quickly brought up to acceptable standards. He relates a humorous incident that pertained to the local Bedouin tribe that inhabited that area. "We were having trouble keeping the native Bedouins off the range, especially at night. One time, I had to helicopter out to have a meeting with the Chief. Since we did all of our practice at night, we had a dangerous situation developing. I tried to explain to him that we were bombing on the range at night and that his people could not hear us coming. I suggested that they not use the range road at all as it would be safer to take the long way around.

"No matter how I tried to explain, it just did not soak in. There were many nights when the guys would have to pull their bombs off the cross hairs to avoid hitting a Bedouin. Most of the times, they were in vehicles crossing the range. On my second visit to the Chief, all he was interested in doing was trying to work up a trade between my 9mm pistol and his old Army Springfield rifle! That old rifle was in great shape and was probably worth a lot of money, but it wasn't worth the grief I would face if I had agreed to the swap! Fortunately, we didn't have any accidents involving the tribesmen and our bombs. As a matter of fact, the range was in such good shape that the B-52 guys that were operating out of Jeddah used it on numerous occasions. It allowed them to practice their long-range missions where they were expected to bomb on time and on target!"

October was a very busy month for the 415th. The training sorties were at full bore and the targets being selected were almost identical to the targets that they would be expected to hit the first few days of the war. They ranged far beyond their bomb range, hitting practice targets all over Saudi Arabia. Even though the pilots felt very confident that they could destroy any target they were assigned, there was still that nagging doubt in the back of their minds as to whether the Stealth technology would really work against the most intense air defenses that any aircraft could possibly face! In the meantime, their sister squadron (the 416th) was taking various scenarios and data sent back to Tonopah by the 415th, running it through a myriad of tests and helping perfect tactics to carry out the most effective missions. All of this period had been extremely tough for the

This shows a good view of the entrance to King Khalid Air Base in Saudi Arabia, located near the city of Khamis Mushait. It was a new airbase built for the sole purpose of housing units of the Saudi Air Force (mainly F-15 Eagles). This was a natural location for the F-117 to operate out of due to its distance from the Iraqi border. The base was down in the extreme southern portion of Saudi which was out of range to the Scud threat. (Ken Huff)

416th Squadron Commander, Lt. Colonel Greg T. Gonyea (Bandit #329), assumed command of his squadron on 10 August 1990, just eight days after Iraq had invaded Kuwait. It was a pressure-packed time frame and even though his squadron did not deploy over to Saudi Arabia until 2 December, the pilots were intensely focused on all of the scenarios that they may be faced with in the war. This was taken at King Khalid Air Base (Khamis Mushait). (Rose Reynolds)

416th in that pilots felt left behind and there was a chance that they would not get into combat if the war did start. They were definitely not happy about the situation!

Captain Mike "Slime" Mahan (Bandit #323), one of the Ghost Rider pilots comments on his squadron's training regimen back at Tonopah. "Preparation for the upcoming war from the viewpoint of the 416th squadron grew rapidly, once the 415th started feeding back some information. Before they did, we didn't have much to go on. Finally during October, we started going after all the info we could get. Most of this was coming directly from our sister squadron. So, when we were flying normal training sorties out of Tonopah, we were trying to move into the same type missions they were working on. We needed to improve on the skills and tactics that we would need if we went over to the middle east. This ended up being not much different from what we had already been working on! Prior to the start of Desert Shield, the tactics, etc. that we had been perfecting out of Tonopah were exactly what we needed to fight in Desert Storm. We didn't have to alter or learn new things in order to accomplish the mission. But, make no mistake about it, we did try to get as much from the 415th as we could and tie that into our training regimen. Once, we all realized that we would be using these things in a war, we went into them with a little more serious mindset! But, as we found out later, nothing can prepare you for the amount of bullets and missiles that we would have to face over Baghdad."

In August 1990, there had been some changes within the Stealth organization. As previously mentioned, there was a change of command at the wing level with Colonel Alton Whitley assuming responsibility on 17 August. One week earlier, the 416th received a new commanding officer, Lt. Colonel Greg T. Gonyea, who officially took over on 10 August from the outgoing commander Lt. Colonel Gerald C. Carpenter. This must have been a difficult transition for both of the new commanders. For the first ten weeks of Gonyea's command, the 416th was heavily involved in assisting the 415th with improvement of tactics and working the kinks out of several scenarios. It was very essential to have everything perfected by the time the war started and at this time, no one really knew when that would be. In the meantime, Colonel Whitley, who had been out of the Stealth program for a few years, returned to Tonopah to be checked out in the aircraft, so he would be able to fly combat missions once the war began.

Sometime during the Thanksgiving holiday in 1990, the 416th received word that it would be deploying over to Saudi Arabia

Shortly after the Iraqi invasion of Kuwait, the "Black Jets" were notified that they would be deploying over to the middle East. It would be the first mass move of the Stealth out of its top secret base at Tonopah, Nevada. This picture shows the 415th Fighter Squadron's arrival at Langley AFB, Virginia en route to Saudi Arabia. All of the 22 aircraft involved were lined up on a dead runway. It was an impressive sight. Not visible in the picture were thousands of people lined up at the fences, holding American flags and giving the "thumbs up." It was an emotional time for the entire country. (Julie Lidie)

to back up the 415th—finally! On 2 December, the squadron's aircraft were flown over to Langley AFB by pilots from the 417th Training Squadron. The aircrews that would make the long flight to the Gulf region flew the first leg in a transport aircraft, which enabled them to get some valuable rest. The 416th did not encounter bad weather early on in the flight as the 415th had done three months earlier. However, there were some pockets of heavy thunderstorms which made it difficult to hang close to the tankers.

Captain Mahan, the Mobility Officer for the squadron, recalls some of the events associated with the move. "On the third of December, we flew all of the squadron aircraft over to Saudi Arabia. Being the Mobility Officer, I had to attend to all the packing and preparations for the move. Our flight over was fourteen and a half hours long. To this day, that was the longest flight I have ever recorded and I have no desire to duplicate it, especially in a single seat fighter! There were thirteen aerial refuelings on the flight. We used KC-10 tankers and there were two of our F-117s assigned to each one. Most of the refuelings were done in total darkness which was what we had done most of our training on. The sun came up as we were over the Azores and it was an impressive view from our altitude."

Each pilot remembers different things about the long flight, some memories are similar and some are not. Another of the "Ghost Riders" pilots, Major Rod L. Shrader (Bandit #312), tells what he remembers and what impressed him during that flight. "I was in the same flight of F-117s as our wing commander, Colonel Al Whitley, on the way over. After about eight hours of the tight quarters inside the cockpit, I was ready to start banging my helmet on the side of the canopy, wanting to get up and stretch! The most spectacular event that I can recall during the crossing was to see the tankers hand us off, at night, in the middle of the Atlantic. It was quite impressive to witness those big KC-10s change out. Being Stealth pilots, we never chattered on the radio much, but we could listen to those guys maneuver into position. It took about thirty minutes and then we were back on the boom.

We did not miss a lick as they were ahead of us doing the swap, in total darkness!! As the sun was coming up, we were over the coast of North Africa and we could see the Nile River ahead of us. I was taken by the beauty of the landscape and the fact that we were getting close to our destination...and then it dawned on me that we still had over four hours of flying time left."

The arrival of the 416th Squadron at Khamis Mushait was a more pleasant experience for the pilots than it had been for members of the 415th three and a half months prior. The base was functioning well, considering that the influx of personnel and equipment had made living quarters extremely tight. However, there was ample space within the protective shelters to easily accommodate the arriving F-117s. The aircrews were swept into a hectic pace of training missions and preparation for that first night of the war — whenever it was to happen. In truth, the action was still almost six weeks away, but as far as the Night Stalkers and Ghost Riders were concerned, it would be the next night! One of the 416th pilots caught up in the fast learning pace was Captain Jeff "Jammer" Moore (Bandit #292). His views on what they had to do was identical to those of his squadron mates. "It was a real shot in the arm to our morale to learn of our deployment to the region. When we arrived in theatre, we had some quick training to do to get ready for, what might be, a war at any time! As you know, the primary targeting device, the FLIR and DLIR, are infrared sensors which work best against contrasting heat signatures. It took a while to get used to the difference in desert practice targets versus stateside training targets. All the while, the evidence against a successful solution to the Iraqi situation diminished as we built up and readied the coalition forces for war."

The prewar routines of both squadrons were pretty well set. The operational side of the squadrons were totally focussed on mission planning and executing the practice sorties. During the final few weeks before the shooting started, every Stealth pilot pretty well knew what the targets were going to be for the first three nights. The changes coming down from Riyadh had been relatively few as far as the first series of missions were concerned. They had to knock out the Iraqi Air Defense and Communications networks, so there were no targets that would supercede these in priority. The pilots knew that they were expected to take out the most dangerous targets all over Iraq. This was an accepted fact by the entire cadre. They would begin with the Command and Control Centers and Key Communications centers. Once the enemy had been blinded, then the Stealth aircrews would methodically work on destroying the nuclear and chemical research, development, production, and storage facilities. These

As Desert Shield got into full swing, this group of Stealth pilots seemed to be in a more relaxed state of mind, especially when this picture was taken. Many of them are brandishing their unloaded 9mm pistols—standard issue to every pilot. The bus in the background was provided by the Saudis for shuttling back and forth from their quarters to the hardened shelters that housed their aircraft. It would be about four months later that they would take their aircraft into Iraq. (Rob Donaldson)

were heavily defended and scattered out all over Iraq. As these fell, a new series of targets would include hardened-aircraft shelters, resupply lines, bridges, etc.

Lt. Colonel Gonyea shares his thoughts on that particular time frame. "Before the war began, every squadron that was based in Saudi Arabia knew what the first three day's targets were. Our Intel knew what had to be taken out early on and that was the way we practiced and it was also the way we executed the missions when we went into combat. Once we had this information, I took our guys and paired them off. They were assigned certain targets and it was handled on a team basis. I spread out the experience level where I had some of my high time, more experienced pilots working the missions with some [who] had less experience. I wanted to make sure that there was no difference between the first night and the second night — experience-wise! This insured that if one of them got sick or something happened that they couldn't fly, the other pilot would be capable of stepping in and doing the other pilot's assignment. It had to be a 'buddy' system and there was to be no 'A' or 'B' team.

"Getting back to our flights up along the border, the types of missions we flew up in this area [were] done to lull the Iraqis into a false sense of security. First, we had to find out if they could see us. If they could, we had to find out what they were capable of doing. By repeating these sorties over and over, if they could see us, then they figured they knew exactly what we were going to do. Then, one of these days, we were going to do something totally different and they were going to be caught off guard and that is exactly what happened on the night of 16 January."

What was about to unfold was absolutely phenomenal and to realize why, you have to understand that it had been 16 years since there had been any type of war that involved the United States military in such a large show of force. First of all, the more experience you have going into any type of competitive endeavor, the better chance you have of winning. According to Colonel Whitley, "In those 'first night' briefings, I only remember three pilots who had experienced combat before: Colonel Klause and myself in Vietnam and Major Rod Shrader, who flew a single mission in an A-10 during the brief conflict in Granada. Maybe there had been others, but none that I recall in the briefings."

It was this fact that made the repetitious practice missions so valuable. As you will see in the Desert Storm Chapter, these young untested pilots delivered precision blows to targets that were in the most heavily defended areas and they did it in three waves per night. This proved the point that if you have to go into battle, there is no limit to how much practice you must do to prepare for it.

Meanwhile, back at Tonopah, the only remaining unit was the 417th Training Squadron commanded by Lt. Colonel Robert Maher. With both of their sister squadrons on the brink of going to war, he provides some insight as to what was going on, at this time, with his squadron. "When I took over the 417th, my main goal was to improve on the combat capabilities of my squadron's pilots. They were all excellent instructors and I wanted them to be every bit as good as the guys who were flying in the operational units. Up to this point, our pilots would grab a mission folder from a pile that we kept and they would fly it to perfection. The problem was that they were hitting the same targets over and over which provided very little training or challenge.

"Through the significant efforts of Captains Ken Huff and Don Chapman, we began to gather target photos and flight plans from the operational guys and we would fly these. This created an entirely new set of targets for us and increased our training and proficiency dramatically. I also required the three pilots to debrief together with heavy emphasis on tape debriefing and bombing accuracy. It became very competitive and usually the one with the lowest score had to buy the drinks in our off time. We were not in the combat zone, but our leadership knew that we were ready if called upon. Although, we had been told that we would not deploy under any circumstances and that the continued training of the new F-117 pilots was to be our top priority! Of course, this would all change during the first couple of days of the war."

During the final stages of Desert Shield, there were a series of practice sorties flown up on the Iraqi border that proved to boost the confidence of each F-117 pilot more than words can describe. Every Stealth pilot who ever strapped in for a combat mission over Iraq always wondered, deep down, if the "stealth" technology would work. Nothing was to be left to chance when the shooting started. The 37th Wing chose to test exactly how good the enemy was going to be and did this by sending fighters along the border to test the Iraqis' reaction. Captain Donaldson remembers the details. "All of our training missions were flown within the borders of Saudi Arabia. On several occasions, we flew all the way up to Iraq (2.5 hours flying time). This was to test their reaction to our presence in the area. It was these flights up to the border that proved to be beneficial and a morale booster for all of us. There were no indications that they were ever aware of our being in the area! However, when other aircraft types (non-stealth), came into this same vicinity, they immediately heated up the Iraqi radar scopes and they would have no surprise effect on the enemy. It was at this time, we all knew that when the war started, we would ease right in on our assigned targets, completely undetected. Our degree of confidence was high.

"Another important facet of those final training sorties was executing numerous hookups with our tankers. We used the exact routine that we would use in the war. Fly up to the border, top off, and then instead of heading east, we would fly back to Khamis. The Iraqis became very comfortable with this. There was one thing we had going against us during this period and also in the first few weeks of the war — unpredictable weather. It would cause us a lot of trouble in identifying our target and also trying to stay close to our tankers in zero/zero visibility. Also, hanging onto the boom at about 300 knots proved to be a handful. This was solved by having the tankers increase their speed. To say we were all ready to take it to Iraq would have been an understatement!"

Chapter Three

The Assault on Fortress Iraq Begins

After five long months of preparation, anticipation, and count-less practice missions at night, the mind games were over and the real thing was staring the Stealth pilots in the face. Up until now, they had all flown their "Night One" assignments, in their minds, over and over again. As far as the 37th Fighter Wing was concerned, Colonel Alton Whitley and his Director of Opera-tions, Colonel Klaus Klause got the notification first. It was early Wednesday morning, 16 January 1991. Major Jerry Leatherman, one of the key figures in the F-117 Mission Planning Cell recalls how he was awaken about 10:00 A.M. after having spent a long night in the MPC. "I was trying to get some sleep after a long night of working the mission assignments for 'Night One.' One of the guys from the Command Post came over, woke me, and said that Colonel Whitley wanted to see me right away. I got up and half dressed, went over to see him. I clearly remember Colonel Whit-ley handing me this piece of paper that said 'Execute Wolf Pack...H-Hour is Zero One Zero One Zulu,' which translates to 3:00 A.M. Baghdad time. I recall there was also some information in the notice about changes in targets, but none of them affected our aircraft. As both Colonels waited for my comments, all I could think of was the line from the Cold War cult film *Dr. Strangelove*, that was credited to the actor Slim Pickens when he received the coded message to launch a nuclear strike on the Soviet Union: 'Well, it looks like we've got the Go Code here!!!' This time, there were no actors in sight, just Stealth pilots, and they had just been given the green light to attack Iraq!

Major Joe Bouley (Bandit #331) was one of the mission planners for the 415th squadron. He and others in the cell, had spent the last few weeks fine-tuning the first night's strike packages. Most

Sunset over Saudi Arabia. This F-117 is part of the first strike package for the night. Many times, these aircraft would take off from Khamis Mushait before dark, but by the time they reached the Iraqi border, the sky would be total darkness. The Stealth never flew over enemy territory in light and only on rare occasions where they had flown long distance missions up on the Turkish border, did they get caught in early morning light before they reached the Saudi border. (Lockheed Martin Skunk Works)

of the "tweaking" of the packages had to do with updated information that had been picked up by Intel concerning particular placement of threats such as Triple-A or SAMs. The exposure to these had to be minimized through constant reworking. His recollections of that day were as follows. "I was hanging around the McDonnell Douglas facilities (pool), when someone came and told me that Colonel Klause wanted to see me right away. I changed into my flying suit and immediately went over, but the Colonel was not in his office. At that time, Major Leatherman walked over and handed me a piece of paper marked 'Top Secret.' It said, 'Execute Desert Storm.' It was for that night and I was shocked for a second. All of this happened about 2:30 P.M.

In short order, I learned that I would not be flying in the first or second wave because I was needed to finish working the missions and integrating the last-minute changes that had just come down. The briefings of the final strike plans would be given by Lt. Colonel Getchell to his 415th squadron and Capt. Troyer to the 416th squadron."

Every member of the Wing remembers exactly what he was doing and where he was when word was received that the war would begin that night. It is like how "older" people can tell you the same thing when they heard that President John F. Kennedy

Once the pilots returned to Khamis after the final sortie of the night, the work was just beginning on the ground. Many of the F-117s were flying two sorties per night. This picture shows one of the crew chiefs riding in the cockpit of his assigned Stealth as it is slowly towed into the hardened-aircraft shelter. By 5 P.M. every day, these aircraft had been serviced and loaded with ordnance for the upcoming first strike of the night. (Guy Aceto / Air Force Association)

had been assassinated. Rob Donaldson tells of how Colonel Whitley called everyone in to the hardened shelter where the briefings were held. "'This is it gentlemen. We are taking it to them tonight!' The atmosphere in the room at the time was very calm, professional, and businesslike. This was exactly what we had been training for and we were ready to go right then, especially the 415th guys who had been at Khamis for so long. It was a relief to all of us."

As this chapter progresses, the reader will note that there is constant reference to "first wave" and "second wave" of Stealth air-

Lt. Colonel Greg Gonyea, 416th Fighter Squadron commanding officer, poses by his Stealth fighter Magic Hammer *before climbing into the cockpit for another night mission over Iraq. Gonyea assumed command of the 416th on 10 August 1990, eight days after Iraq had invaded Kuwait. The squadron encountered horrible weather on the long flight across the Atlantic Ocean en route to the new base in Saudi Arabia. (Greg Gonyea)*

A large percentage of the credit for the Stealth's success in Desert Storm was due to the professionalism and dedication of the maintenance personnel. These two crew chiefs pose with their squadron commander, Lt. Colonel Gonyea in a hardened-aircraft shelter at Khamis Mushait during the Gulf War. As far as the crew chiefs were concerned, the aircraft belonged to them. (G.T. Gonyea)

craft. In reality, there is no such thing as a "wave" of aircraft, at least not in the Stealth world! The F-117s would launch in twos and once they were airborne, each aircraft did its own thing. Pilots worked together only when they were dependent on the tankers (up to the border and then back). Once the fuel was topped off, each pilot had an agenda. Even if both aircraft had targets that were in the vicinity of each other, each pilot had a specific route to fly. There were, however, a few alterations to this concept, especially after the plans began using much more complicated and sophisticated tactics, but that will be covered later in the book. As you read about "waves" in some of the first-

Major Joseph R. Bouley, one of the 415th pilots, has finished briefings and is preparing to climb into his F-117 for another night mission into Iraq. Not only did he fly his share of the sorties, but he was also the squadron's Chief of Mission Planning. When the 415th deployed to Saudi Arabia during the early stages of Desert Shield, he was relatively new to the program compared to other pilots in the squadron. His total F-117 time was slightly over 50 hours. All of this changed rapidly once the Stealth's training regimen was set up at Khamis Mushait. (Joe Bouley)

hand accounts, it will be easier to understand what the pilots are talking about. A wave of F-117s were simply a set number of aircraft that had launched at approximately the same time, but each went its own way.

On the night of 16-17 January 1991, one of the most complicated, well-executed aerial battle plans in the history of warfare, unfolded in the form of Desert Storm. At the remote F-117 base, it was like a rehearsed symphony, with very little talking, only the whine of the engines as the ominous black jets moved as they

Major Rod Shrader, one of the 416th Fighter Squadron "Ghost Rider" pilots is shown here with his assigned F-117 during Desert Storm. His aircraft was named Mystic Warrior *by his crew chief. By the time Shrader left the Stealth program, he had accumulated over 500 hours in the F-117. However, his most significant cockpit time was done in the A-10 with 2,500 hours. A large number of the Stealth pilots who fought in Desert Storm had experience in the Warthog.* (Rod Shrader)

were timed to do, all in perfect harmony. Every thing was done on timing as the only radio chatter was between a crew chief and his pilot, if there was a slight problem. The Wing leadership was staggered in the mission schedule as one person remained on the ground to handle anything that might crop up. This meant that when Colonel Whitley was flying, his Director of Operations, Colonel Klause was on the ground and vice versa.

These three officers represent "upper management" for both the 37th Wing and the 416th Fighter Squadron. Left to right: Major Kim Field-stad, Operations Officer for the 416th; Wing Commander Colonel Al Whitley; and 416th Squadron Commander Lt. Colonel Greg Gonyea. They are standing in front of Col. Whitley's assigned F-117 at Khamis Mushait during the war. (G.T. Gonyea)

This is a good profile shot of "Team Stealth" taken right after Desert Storm ended. These troops represent a number of combined specialties that made the F-117 effective. In the middle is 416th Squadron commander, Lt. Colonel Gonyea. This was taken at Khamis Mushait AB in Saudi Arabia. A significant number of the aircraft would remain at this base for quite some time as a precautionary measure to insure stability in the region. In the few years after this was taken, the F-117s were forced to deploy from the states over to Kuwait on numerous occasions to calm Saddam's sword rattling and threats. (G.T. Gonyea)

Major Leatherman can now look back with a smile at the main briefing before the "show" started, but it was serious business at the time. "The funny thing about that first night of the war, during a normal mass briefing before the war started, it would take close to thirty minutes. I remember Joe Bouley getting up there in front of us guys that were on the first go. He starts going through the brief and its over in about ten minutes. We already knew what our targets were and had gone over it in our minds countless times. There was nothing new to be talked about except this time, we were going to be shot at! Every one of the pilots took his time, making sure he had all of his survival equip-

Major Wesley Wyrick, one of the original cadre of 415th pilots to deploy to Khamis Mushait in August 1990, poses on the ladder of his Stealth fighter #821, during Desert Storm. The aircraft was named Sneak Attack *and during the course of the hostilities, it flew a total of 32 combat sorties. By the time Major Wyrick finished his tour in the F-117, he had accumulated slightly over 700 hours of flight time in the Nighthawk. Some of the missions he logged were over seven hours in duration and these took him across Iraq and almost up to the Turkish border.* (Wesley Wyrick)

ment and Form-70s (where everything looked just like the pilots remembered it). Then I recall a bunch of us just went out in front of a hangar, smoking a cigarette. To me, this just didn't have what you would call a sense of urgency that most people would picture in their minds. It was very businesslike and it was exactly what we were there for! One of our favorite sayings was 'You know, the quickest way home is through Baghdad!'"

The first wave, which consisted of ten aircraft, launched at 12:26 A.M. If there was any confusion within the ranks, it was invisible to the naked eye. All of this precision movement had to be the classic example of "Practice makes perfect!" This impressive scene can best be told by one of the pilots who witnessed it from the ground as it unfolded with the first ten aircraft coming out and taking up their positions. Major Wesley Wyrick (Bandit

These pilots flew several sorties together in a four-ship, including a few deep into northern Iraq near the Turkish border. On these missions, they had to bring their tankers over enemy territory in order to receive enough fuel to get back out to the border again. These routes usually were the longest missions flown by the Stealth in Desert Storm, with a duration of about seven and a half hours. Left to right: Captain Phil McDaniel, Captain Neil McAskill, Major Rod Shrader (sitting), and Captain John Savidge. (Rod Shrader)

Colonel Alton Whitley, 37th Fighter Wing Commander, is shown taxiing out for another mission. Note the numerous mission symbols painted under the canopy rail. Whitley stated that the most memorable aspect of his first mission over Baghdad was how the city seemed to have a dull orange glow from a distance, due to the intense Triple-A. Even on 100% oxygen, he remembers that he could still smell the aroma of gunpowder from the exploding shells all around him. (Lockheed Martin Skunk Works)

#330) was the 415th Assistant Operations Officer and while the first ten ships assembled for takeoff, it was his duty to be down there with them in a capacity of what he describes as the "ramp rat." "It was extremely interesting to watch something as complicated as this, come off like clockwork. For all of us on the ground, it was a tense period. Once all of the guys got airborne, we had no more contact with them, so we had to depend on CNN to find out how we did. We knew exactly where every aircraft was headed and the second they were to be over their targets. It was amazing how well it went. We had a group of very disciplined pilots. Every thing we did was based on precise timing. The pilots came out to their aircraft, got in, started the engines, and waited for their time to move out into position.

"From that point on it was like watching a ballet at night. Aircraft were taxiing out at certain times, coming from all over the base, from opposite sides of the runway. Each knew when he was to move out and there was no radio transmission between the tower and our F-117s. They would line up side-by-side at the end of the runway and at a set time, they would start rolling down the runway and then another pair would pull up into position. It was all radio with no radio transmissions 'com out.' It would be radio out to ground operations, radio out for depar-

When the Stealth aircraft began nocturnal precision bombing missions against targets in downtown Baghdad, they were facing thousands of gun barrels pointing straight up. It was probably the most heavily defended city in the history of warfare. These captured Iraqi anti-aircraft weapons were very mobile and could be moved many miles each night. Allied Intelligence did a superb job of pinpointing a large number of them so that the data could be processed into the mission planning regimen. It was a miracle that the F-117s didn't even receive a scratch. (K.D. Boyer)

Three combat-seasoned Stealth pilots from the 416th Fighter Squadron relax with a good cigar and a little time off right after the war ended. Left to right are: Captain Michael "Slime" Mahan, Captain Raymond "Shredder" Lynott, and Major Michael "Rico" Christensen. It was Mahan who dropped the last bomb of the war on the last combat sortie, against a rocket motor factory. During Storm, he flew two different F-117s on a regular basis: Mystic Warrior *and* Double Down. *(Mike Mahan)*

The deep-penetrating effect of a 2,000-pound GBU-27 bomb doesn't look impressive on video tape or from a satellite picture. Most of this hardened-aircraft shelter (HAS) appears to be intact except for a large hole in the center. It was the amount of destruction on the contents of the shelter that told the story. On many occasions, Intel would ask that a HAS be hit again, when the Stealth mission planners knew that it had been destroyed. (Rob Donaldson)

ture, then go up and hit the tanker ... radio out. The first transmissions from the aircraft would be when they were heading south after the strike, usually at the Iraqi/Saudi border."

Actually, the number of Stealth aircraft that were used that first night was only a very small percentage of the Coalition Strike Force, yet they took out the most heavily defended targets in and around Baghdad. To better understand what the F-117 accomplished, you have to have an idea of just how overwhelming the Force was. Phase I of the Gulf Air War was scheduled to begin precisely at 3 A.M. Its objective was crystal clear; achieve instant air superiority, destroy Iraq's Strategic capabilities, and disrupt all of Saddam Hussein's Command and Control. The Stealth had nothing to do with sweeping the Iraqi Air Force out of the sky, but it sure played havoc on its Command and Control. By midnight on 17 January, the land-based Coalition aircraft had flown over 750 combat sorties and the U.S. Navy logged 228 sorties, launching from six super carriers that were operating from the Red Sea and the Arabian Gulf. If you included the AH-64 Apache helicopters, there were fifteen different combat aircraft involved from just the American side of the massive effort. The world had not seen a military operation like this since D-Day in June 1944.

In recent years, there have been a few stories published that indicated the Tomahawk Land-Attack Missiles (TLAMs) might

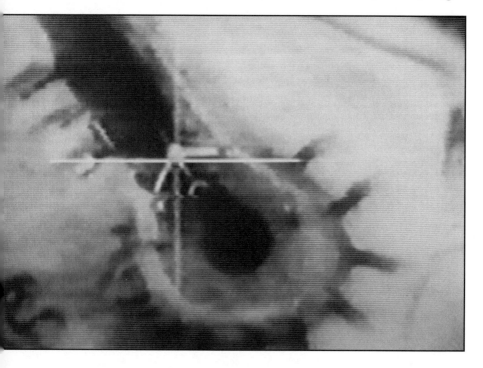

A dramatic photo taken from the video camera of an F-117 as it puts the crosshairs on an unsuspecting Russian built Tu-16 "Badger" bomber parked in a revetment at El Taqaddum Airfield. The Intelligence people determined that a certain number of these bombers had been loaded with chemical weapons and were to be delivered at dawn the next day. The mission planning cell at Khamis Mushait hastily re-rolled a mission and sent two F-117s after these bombers, using the GBU-10s. They were destroyed before first light. (U.S. Air Force)

Right after the Gulf War ended, the pilots were able to get some much needed rest and relaxation although they were on constant alert to react to any aggressive moves that Iraq might make. The 416th Squadron personnel at Khamis Mushait Air Base is shown here. Second from the right, standing, is squadron commander Lt. Colonel Greg Gonyea. The 415th Squadron was the first to rotate back to the states because it had been in theatre since August 1990. Between the two squadrons, the F-117s were tasked with destroying over 40% of the total number of strategic targets assigned to the coalition air arm. (Rod Shrader)

have been the first to strike Iraq. Beyond the shadow of a doubt, it was the F-117s that drew first blood in the Gulf War. If it had not been for their ability to execute an assignment with precision timing, then they might have been second in that contest. For a fact, it was Major Greg Feest (Bandit #261) of the 415th Squadron who dropped the first bomb of Desert Storm. Major Bouley states, "To set the records straight, the Tomahawks did not make the first hits in Iraq. Official records that I have had the opportunity to read, state that the first wave of Cruise Missiles struck Baghdad at 3:05 A.M. Two of our F-117s bombed radar sites outside of the city at 2:51 A.M. At 3 A.M. sharp, we had eight jets hit downtown Baghdad. Precisely one hour later, a second wave of F-117s (ten aircraft) hit more targets in the same vicinity as the first wave."

When the planning for the first night's attacks was in its final stages, there was some worry about the close five minute timing between the Stealth and Tomahawk strikes. Timing was not a problem to the Stealth pilots and they got in, did their job, and were out of the area before the first missiles struck. In the span of five minutes, all eight aircraft entered the airspace over the city of Baghdad, found their targets, dropped their ordnance, and exited the area. By the time the Cruise Missiles came overhead, you could literally walk on the Triple-A (anti-aircraft artillery) that was being thrown up.

During the first ten minutes of the assault on "Fortress Baghdad," it was a few F-117s and several TLAMs that stirred up the hornet's nest. Major Feest and his wingman Captain David Francis (Bandit #317), hit a critically important IOC (Interceptor Operations Center) which was approximately fifty miles inside of Iraq. This target was the key to opening up a corridor for conventional aircraft to go through. Their safety could only be enhanced by taking it out. It was well-camouflaged and fully contained within a protective, hardened bunker. This facility was the key link between radar units located along the Saudi Arabian border and the main air defense headquarters in Baghdad. Feest's bomb hit dead center, penetrating the bunker and blowing the doors out. This was only his first target. The second bomb was slated for an airfield in the western part of Iraq. A short time later, this target was destroyed and both pilots faced the long flight back to Khamis Mushait.

The two F-117s that made the initial attack that first night set off a fast and furious pace that would be followed by the other Nighthawks that entered Iraqi airspace right after them. Captain Francis, who was known to his fellow pilots as "Dogman," recalls the details of that first night's strike that helped open up the floodgates for an armada of other aircraft types. "We stepped out to our jets ridiculously early! I think we gave ourselves an extra thirty minutes or so, just to insure that if we could find any problems, we would be able to get them fixed without being late for takeoff. As we were getting ready to step out the door, our

Flight Management Chief MSgt Ed O'Neill, gave us each a white envelope. I looked inside and it contained a couple of 8x10 American flags, apparently provided by Lockheed. He wanted me to keep them in the cockpit for the mission. We went right out and boarded our 'shuttle' bus that would take us across the base to our airplanes. As each pilot got off, he shook hands with all the others. In the back of our minds, we all wondered who would return and who would not! After all, we had been told to expect two or three of our F-117s to go down on the first night!

The Stealth pilots were shuttled around the big base at Khamis in Saudi buses like this one. Left to right: Captain Rob "Robsan" Donaldson and Captain John "Doc" Savidge. Both were assigned to the 415th Squadron and they flew in the first wave of Stealth aircraft that came over from Tonopah in August. Personnel from the Wing were, for the most part, kept within the confines of the base for safety reasons. There was always the threat of terrorist activity. (Rob Donaldson)

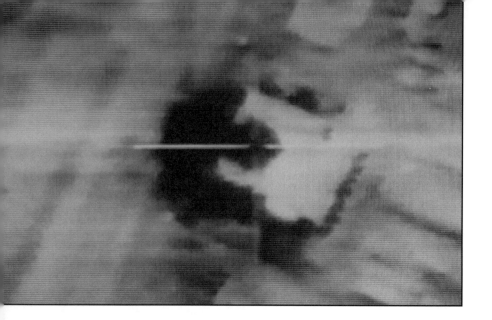

This was taken through the crosshairs in an F-117 over a doomed target. Note the GBU-27 had penetrated through the top of the structure with a delayed fuse. As it got down close to ground level, it exploded, blowing two sides of the building. It is difficult to tell if this was a hardened-aircraft shelter or a building that housed production facilities. If it was a normal building, without reinforced protection, a GBU-10 would have done the same amount of damage. Both bomb types weighed in at 2,000 pounds and were laser guided to the target. (Lockheed Martin Skunk Works)

"When I arrived at my aircraft, my crew chief, Sgt. Jerry Falby was waiting for me. My plane was #821 which carried the name *Sneak Attack*. I knew it had been picked for this mission due to its very good stealth signature, but that could be taken away in a heartbeat by one missing piece of RAM (radar absorbent material). I went over the outside of the aircraft thoroughly with a flashlight. This inspection showed no problem, so I climbed in and started the engines. Everything checked out perfectly. Now, all I had to do was wait 35 more minutes before I could taxi out. While sitting up in the cockpit, I said several prayers and they were mostly about hoping that all our guys returned from their missions and that I would not screw up on my deliveries and let the others down.

"Finally, we took off. Everything went just like we had trained. We found the tanker on time, got our gas, and started heading north. Shortly after the first refueling, my FLIR went blank! This wasn't good! The 'forward looking infrared' was used for finding the target well forward of the delivery point. From the altitudes we were using on this mission, the target did not appear in the DLIR until less than one minute to when we pickled our bombs. For big, easy to identify targets, there would have been no problem, but for my first one (an earth-covered bunker) it would be cutting it very close!! I tried all of the things to get it working again; turning it off, letting it cool, and turning it back on again. I did this at least five times, with absolutely no success. I finally

While Saddam Hussein may have spent a lot of dollars on his war machine, he never cut back on his expenditures for state-of-the-art hardened-aircraft shelters. They were built to withstand everything but a direct nuclear blast. However, it was the deep penetrating GBU-27 (2,000-pound) bombs that were able to destroy most of them. This hangar at Tallil was wrecked by an F-117's bomb during a late-night raid. Everything within the hangar was also destroyed. (Jeff Moore)

decided to go with what I had. If something had to break, I would rather it be my FLIR than my DLIR. If the latter had gone out, I would have turned around and returned to base because there would have been no way to point my laser at the target which meant that the bomb would go 'stupid.'

"We took our final top-off of fuel and dropped away from the tanker. Feest left first and I watched as his dim lights went out and he disappeared into the darkness. One minute later, I followed. My concentration was fixed on running through the seven-step stealth line check. I must have double checked my lights

The 416th Squadron's "A" Flight slows down long enough to pose for the camera. Left to right: Captain Daniel DeCamp, Major Mike Christensen, Lt. Colonel Greg Gonyea (416th C.O.), Captain Jeff Moore, Captain Ray Lynott, and Captain Neil McAskill. This was taken at Khamis Mushait. (Jeff "Jammer" Moore)

Captain Jeff "Jammer" Moore (Bandit #292) stands by his assigned F-117. This was a/c #834 that had the name Necromancer *painted on its bay door. During the brief course of the Gulf War, #834 flew 34 combat missions over Iraq and Kuwait. Captain Moore logged numerous missions over the highly defended Iraqi airfields at H-2 and H-3. (Jeff "Jammer" Moore)*

Even when the pilots were not scheduled to fly missions, much of the time they were either in Mission Planning or hanging around the shelters and their aircraft. This photo shows Major Miles Pound posing on the bomb cart that has two 2,000-pound "smart" bombs on it. As shown here, the spartan conditions on the outside of the shelters, proved that most, if not all, of the equipment, tools, and ordnance was safely stowed on the inside of the shelters. (Ken Huff)

switch a dozen times! It was poorly designed; a three position switch, with off in the middle. If you accidentally clicked it down instead of to the center, your lights were on dim. It was almost impossible to see your wing lights from the cockpit and very hard to bend your head down under the canopy rail and see the switch position, so I flicked it up and down several times to insure that I was feeling it in the middle position.

"We had a pretty short run to our target of not more than fifteen minutes. I was very careful to stay right on my timing, because I didn't want to get too close to my lead. I couldn't do much searching for the target without my FLIR, so I looked out of the cockpit a lot. It was pitch black in front of the aircraft. At precisely 02:51 A.M., Feest's bomb hit, which put him nine minutes ahead of the first strikes against Baghdad. I saw his bomb hit in the upper portion of my DLIR screen, which gave me an excellent pointer to my target, since I knew where my bunker was in relation to his. Suddenly, I noticed a lot of white flashes in the air in front of me. His bomb blast had alerted the Iraqi gunners that an attack was underway and the Triple-A was coming up. It seemed like it was pretty heavy, but it was my first experience at getting shot at. In the days to come, I would find out what heavy Triple-A was really like!

This is a grim reminder of what a GBU-10 or GBU-27 could do to an Iraqi hangar. The only thing left standing was a single support beam for the roof. Notice all the burned debris from the walls, roof, and contents that were within the confines of the shelter when the bomb penetrated the roof and exploded. Most Iraqi aircraft that were in the shelters were damaged beyond repair. This was taken at As Salman North Airfield right after the war ended. (Luke Atwell)

"I studied my screen intently, and as I finally located my bunker in that sea of sand, I pressed the pickle button. I could feel the bomb bay doors open and the sudden jolt as the bomb came out. Then, I just concentrated on holding the crosshairs right on the target. About four seconds before impact, it became apparent that I was tracking the left side of the bunker instead of the top. An adjustment was made immediately and the bomb hit right on the roof. It looked just like all the bombs I had dropped during those countless practice missions ... a black star erupted in the center of my scope, but I was able to see smoke coming out of

Iraq had weapons storage facilities scattered all over the country. Many of these were never picked up by Coalition Intelligence. The ones that were, however, were taken out promptly by a wide variety of aircraft types which included the night flying Nighthawks. This picture shows one of ninety such intact storage facilities that were examined and destroyed after the war ended. (Luke Atwell)

This is another view of the many arsenals that had escaped destruction during the 43-day war. There were close to one hundred of these facilities that were discovered and destroyed by the 82nd Airborne Division right after the war. The plastic bags that are on top of some of the ammo crates are explosive charges that have been set by the demolition troops. Moments after this was taken, the entire building went up in a massive explosion. (Luke Atwell)

the doors of the bunker. Obviously, it was a perfect hit. This was a tremendous relief to know that I had done my job and that the F-15E Strike Eagles behind me, could get through to their targets. I quickly turned west and headed for my second target."

The initial barrage of Cruise missiles were fired from four warships that were within range of Iraq. The first salvo was launched from the Cruiser USS *San Jacinto* on station in the Red Sea. It was fired at 1:30 A.M. and had to cover 700 miles to impact. Its airspeed was about 450 knots and the timing was set for 3:05 A.M. The other ships that were involved in the opening waves of Tomahawks were the USS *Bunker Hill* and the battleships, USS *Missouri* and USS *Wisconsin*.

The destructive capabilities of the F-117's GBU-27 is shown in this picture. Note that this hardened-aircraft shelter was probably one of the newer bomb-proof types that Iraq had. The bomb penetrated the roof and created such as explosion inside that the heavy concrete / steel doors were blown out. Pieces of the doors hit the Soviet built "Hip" helicopter which had been parked beside the shelter, destroying it. Due to the evidence of a massive fire within the structure, there must have been several fueled aircraft inside. (Luke Atwell)

The previous paragraph only outlines what was slated for the city of Baghdad. The total strike package that was unleashed by the Coalition air arm was impressive, to say the least! Between 3:00 A.M. and about 5:25 A.M. (Baghdad time), approximately 400 attack aircraft went after more than 100 targets all across Iraq and Kuwait. All of these were conventional, non-stealthy types that had to have protection. This was provided by the jamming EF-111 Ravens and EA-6B Prowlers along with the F-4G Wild Weasel radar suppression specialists. Enough time was allowed before this force went into action, so the F-117s could get in and blind Iraq's air defense systems, making it much safer for the "shooters" to take out their targets.

As the first wave of Nighthawks were heading back toward the Saudi border, the F-15C Eagles and F-14 Tomcats were setting up their protective corridors to handle any Iraqi airborne response. There was an effort to respond by the MiGs and when the curtain had come down after the first day of the war, eight of their interceptors had been shot down. Six by the Air Force and two by the Navy. The 33rd Tactical Fighter Wing (F-15C) drew first blood by shooting down a MiG-29 at 3:10 A.M. and following it up with two F-1 Mirages at 3:54 A.M. None of the above mentioned Coalition "shooters" were assigned any targets within Baghdad as this was to be the F-117s domain.

Even with all the rehearsal and preparation that went into Day-1 of the war, there is always something, unforeseen, that can go wrong. In any war, it is known as Murphy's Law. One of the

The remnants of a MiG-23 rests beside one of the many destroyed shelters at Tallil Airfield. More than likely, this Iraqi fighter was destroyed by a bomb that had been redirected by a Stealth pilot after it had already left the aircraft. During the second and third week of the war, the hardened-aircraft shelters were being destroyed at such a fast rate that the Iraqis started parking some of the aircraft on the outside in hopes they would be spared. This was taken a few days after the Gulf War ended. (Luke Atwell)

Wing's mission planners was assigned one of the most important targets for that first night and it almost didn't come off, but when it worked out, the results were spectacular. Captain Marcel Kerdavid explains what happened at the beginning and how it ended. "My primary target was to be the tall Arquark Communications Tower that resembled the Seattle Space Needle. I went out to my aircraft when it came time to start engines, my right one would not start. I tried everything and valuable time was ticking away. Fortunately, we had a spare set up and when it became apparent that it wasn't going to start, I jumped into the spare. I went right out and got airborne in an effort to keep my timing perfect. There was only one thing wrong with the aircraft I had and that was the fact it was loaded with two GBU-27s. The bomb

The main gate to Tallil Airfield shows very few signs of a war. The portrait of Saddam Hussein and the "Gate Guard" on a pedestal remain relatively intact. After Night One of the war, there were very few civilian types in or around the base. It was pounded nightly by Coalition forces. However, the Triple-A activity remained intense for quite some time even though the base had been rendered inoperable. RAF Tornados and F-111Fs had completely destroyed the main runway and taxiways. (Luke Atwell)

that I needed for the tower was a GBU-10. This bothered me on the way in because the -27 was a penetrator and it could easily punch right through the narrow tower and out the other side before it exploded.

"Our munitions experts had determined that the GBU-10, if well placed at the top of the tower, would explode on impact, destroying all the critical equipment that was positioned there, thus knocking it out of commission. Regardless of the situation, I went with what I had. It was easy to locate and as I got it in the crosshairs, I dropped the bomb perfectly. I didn't hang around to observe the results because I had another target to hit. The next night, I was viewing the tape from another F-117 sortie that had

An ill-fated Iraqi Jaguar was damaged by flying debris from a nearby shelter destroyed by a Stealth GBU. The camouflage netting that had been thrown over the aircraft was of no use against the bomb blast a few meters away. The damage was enough to keep the aircraft grounded until the war ended. At that time, the 82nd Airborne Division sent its demolition crews in and this Jag was blown up. (Luke Atwell)

A member of the 82nd Airborne enters the burned-out ruins of an Iraqi hardened-aircraft shelter hit by a GBU-27. The fireball that was contained within the structure built up so much pressure that it blew the massive doors open. The aircraft that were parked inside were burned to the ground. Note the amount of debris that was blown out. (Luke Atwell)

taken out a target next to where the Arquark Tower was and I was amazed!! The tower was actually gone. What had happened was that the GBU-27 had hit perfectly, penetrating only one side of the tower and not having enough energy to go out the other side, it dropped down inside the tower, plummeting as its timed fuse was about to trigger the bomb. At a certain distance inside the tower, it exploded and the entire tower disintegrated. Strangely enough, the -27 worked better than the -10 would have. This target had been the main communications facility in the center of Baghdad. Jerry Leatherman and I had worked long, hard hours working on the plans for this mission and we sure didn't factor any mechanical problems into the equation!"

Wing Commander Colonel Whitley and 416th Squadron Commander Lt. Colonel Gonyea were both flying in the second wave of aircraft that launched that first night. By this time, all hell had erupted over Baghdad and anyone who watched CNN will attest to the density of the ground fire. The first bombs to drop on the city had triggered the non-stop shower of lead. It was one thing to watch it on television and another to bear witness to it as your aircraft ran the gauntlet. Colonel Whitley gives his views on the first mission he flew over Baghdad. "The most memorable aspect of my first operational mission was the density of the defenses over the city. Frankly, the briefing, ground procedures, takeoff, tanker rendezvous, ingress, target attacks, second tanker hookup, and return to Khamis were no different from any other normal mission. What I remember most on that first night were the explosions at and above my ingress altitude, as well as the intensity and density of the defenses below me! I will never forget how Baghdad appeared as a dull orange glow on the horizon at a distance, yet became an intense fireworks display as I

A close-up view of an undetected Iraqi Ammunition Storage facility that was visited by the 82nd Airborne after the war. Explosive charges were set and the entire building was detonated. Note the stencil markings on the cases of ammunition. (Luke Atwell)

approached. The closer I got, the more I doubted our ability to fly through the defenses and survive! Over the city, the bright flashes illuminated my cockpit and I could feel the concussions and hear the explosions. Eventually, the skies became so saturated with enemy fire that the flow of 100% oxygen in the cockpit could not overcome the aroma of gunpowder. Quite frankly, I held little hope that all of our aircraft and pilots had made it through unscathed. This was an eye-opening experience, like nothing I had ever seen before."

For most of the thirty pilots who flew into Iraq during Day One, the memories are still vividly etched in their minds. Since no other coalition aircraft flew any missions inside of the "ring of fire,"

Lt. Colonel Robert Maher kneels in front of two deadly GBU-27 bombs that have been loaded on one of the F-117's at Khamis. Maher was the commanding officer of the training squadron (417th) that had remained behind at Tonopah. Right after the Gulf War began, several of the 417th's instructor pilots were brought over to help with the work load. Maher came over and became the Assistant Director of Operations under Colonel Klaus Klause. (Scott Stimpert)

then only those few F-117 pilots can ever relate what their feelings were when they flew into that ominous orange glow over Baghdad. All of them were aware of the danger, but none faltered. This fact is reflected in what they accomplished by the time the war had ended. Jerry Leatherman had a few things to say about his first mission. "As far as my first mission was concerned, it went exactly the way I thought it would. I know a lot of our guys talk about all the stuff that was going on around us and I was aware that we could be killed. But, my worst fear was screwing up because so many of the others in the Wing were depending on me and besides, I didn't want to have to show my video tape to anyone if I messed up the mission! I don't know what the others saw on the outside of the cockpit, but when I was on my bomb run, I looked out of the cockpit and it reminded me of a scene that was like a screensaver on the computer, where all the fireworks were going off all over the screen and yet, there was no sound! You could hear the pops every now and then, but mostly it was silent and very colorful.

"Actually, there were two distractions for me when I started my bomb run to the target; I remember looking down at my IRADS (Infrared Acquisition and Designation System) and saying, 'That can't be my target because the cursor is laying right on it!!!' So, I went and checked one of the offsets that we were using on this particular mission. One of them that I was using was the large Iraqi War Memorial that they had built to honor all of their military personnel that had been killed in the Iran/Iraq War. Anyway, this structure sits out by itself, so when I clicked over and sure enough it went right to that and then I clicked from that back over to the target and sure enough, I was dead on it. At that moment, I thought that this was going to be easy, so I relaxed just long enough to glance outside of the cockpit! What I saw would be difficult to describe. Then, I realized that I had better concentrate on my bomb delivery and quit looking outside! This was an unusual mission for the F-117 in that both of my bombs were slated for the same target, so I didn't have to worry about getting over to another area. Both of my bombs hit right on the target, which was the AT&T Building in Baghdad."

When the first bomb impacted in Baghdad, the sky was lit up with every type of Triple-A and small arms fire. There had to be hundreds of non-military types that were on the rooftops and out in the streets firing up in the air. The population figures for Baghdad (census of 1987) showed 3,845,000 residents within the city. One of the pilots equated his experience over this heavily defended area as trying to run through the middle of a lawn sprinkler and not get a drop of water on you! The tactic used by that first group of F-117s was to come in over the target area in close trail. The tail-end Charlie (Ship #8) would hit his objective with about a minute left to get out of the way of the incoming TLAMs.

Rob Donaldson was somewhere in that inbound stream of F-117s and he gives his impression of what he saw and how some of their future tactics were to be changed because of the experience gained during that short five minute span. "About the time that we were in our final approach over Baghdad, the Iraq radars that were still up, were picking up our gathering conventional aircraft back on the border (F-4s, F-16, EA-6Bs, EF-111s, etc.) and they were relaying this information back into Baghdad. All of us following the lead ship into the targets were met with a firestorm of Triple-A and SAMs. They were shooting blindly as they had no radar lock or visuals on anything. As we came through it, you could see the intermittent explosions of bombs from the Stealths that were in front of us. All of us on the first round were taking out the C-3 targets (Command & Control & Communications). I got some excellent hits with my two bombs, but there was one hit that sticks out in my mind and that was the one that was assigned to Marcel Kerdavid — the Arquark Communications Tower. It was a very difficult target to hit, but he destroyed it with one well placed GBU-27.

"We learned a few very valuable lessons that first night. Mainly that we had our aircraft coming in trail, one behind the other, attacking targets over the city. Once the first bombs went off, every gun on the ground was pointed straight up and fired. This equated to a lot of lead. The further the F-117 was back in the formation, the higher the risk factor was of being hit. Our tactics

The accuracy of the F-117 at a wide range of altitudes was uncanny. Although this Iraqi aircraft shelter seems to be in relatively good shape, its contents have been totally destroyed and both ends have been blown out. The most significant thing to be noticed in the photo is the hole in the roof. The bomb hit dead center, penetrated through the roof and exploded amidst the aircraft parked inside. The black circle around the hole indicates the massive secondary explosion that was probably generated from aircraft fuel and ordnance inside. (Jeff "Jammer" Moore)

and procedures were modified somewhat in that we would hit a multitude of targets in Baghdad, but it would be at the same time. This meant that all of the bombs would impact about the same time, so within a minute, we had left the area. These basic changes stayed in place for the duration of the war."

The flying time from Khamis Mushait to Baghdad was slightly over three hours. However, sometimes it was more depending on the route that was planned. Very seldom did the Stealth planners assign a direct route into the city (explained later in the mission planning chapter.) So, at the very best, the pilots who were flying this assignment could plan on about six hours in the cockpit. This was markedly better than the flight time from Langley AFB to Saudi Arabia, but at least on the long flight over, no one was shooting at you!

Captain Scott Stimpert eases into his assigned aircraft shelter at Khamis after finishing his "end-of-tour" mission. Waiting on him with a "special surprise" are left to right, Jon Boyd and Jim Mastny (with hose). Note the long row of mission symbols that have been painted on Stimpert's aircraft. The F-117 force represented only 2.5% of the total number of aircraft that were committed to the Gulf War, but they got in and destroyed 95% of the key assets within the city of Baghdad. (Scott Stimpert)

All of the F-117s based at Khamis during Desert Storm, had art-work painted on the inside of their bay doors. Crew chiefs used the artwork as a form of personal expression which gave each aircraft a distinct personality. Major Rod "Hawkeye" Shrader (Bandit #312) of the 416th Squadron talks about his aircraft and some of the quirks it had. He flew it on the first night of the war and was very successful against two separate targets. "My assigned ship was named 'Mystic Warrior.' It was aircraft #841 and very few of the pilots enjoyed flying it because it had the world's most sensi-tive tracker (finger button). Once you got used to it, the target could easily be pinpointed. You always knew which way the track-er was going to drift and how to adjust your finger to make sure you followed the target o.k. The plane had an excellent record during the war while logging eighteen combat sorties and I don't think it was down even once for maintenance problems.

"As far as my first combat mission that first night went, my tar-gets were to be the Iraqi Air Force HQ building and a command bunker. Both of these were located in Baghdad and they were very close together. I think I had a time gap of one and a half min-utes between drops. The ride up to the border with the tankers was uneventful, but what really stuck in my mind was coming up on the city. We were in the second wave to hit, which put us right after the TLAMs struck. By this time, they were mad and ready for us and we sure didn't have the element of surprise going for us like the 415th did on the first strike. I was about thirty minutes from the city and the visibility over the desert was phenomenal. In the back of my mind, I knew all the lights in Baghdad would be off, but for some reason they were on ... at least that is what I thought. As I got closer, I realized that the lights were all ground muzzle flashes from the Triple-A! My plan called for a counter-clockwise route around the city to come in from the northwest and come out in the southeast sector. As I circled the city, the vol-ume of fire coming up was absolutely unbelievable.

"In my mind, I had figured that finding my first target was going to be a little difficult, but as I turned the corner off my IP to go to the target, I had damn good INS on my system and the cursor was laying right on top of the building. I went to my offset point just to confirm and I kept on looking when it finally dawned on me that my cursor was dead center. I dropped my GBU-27 down through the center of the building (down at least eight stories) and created a tremendous explosion, blowing out all four sides of the building! The video was good enough to be released to CNN for viewing on television. Coming off the first target straight to the next one, I had the throttles at max. It was extremely difficult to find because it was a partially buried bunker. Finally, with only about 30 seconds to go, I found it, released the bomb, but I never saw it impact. Although the return flight was quiet, I could not help but wonder how many of our guys had been shot down. There just didn't seem to be any way we could have all gotten through it, but we did. When I finally got hooked up on the tanker, I was able to converse with someone and they confirmed that we had gotten everybody out and no one was lost."

At this early point in the war (Night-One), it is common knowledge that the 37th had two fully complemented squadrons at Khamis. But, what about the third squadron that remained behind at Tonopah? First of all, it was a designated training squadron (the 417th), that had always been tasked with providing replacement pilots to the 415th and 416th as they were needed. So, they would not have a large number of combat-qualified pilots who were waiting to be called up. However, they did have a number of qualified instructor pilots who could hold their own with any of the others. In the first few hours of the war, these pilots were notified to stand by for an immediate move to Khamis Mushait. In other words, the CENTCOM leadership at Riyadh had predicted significant losses for the Stealth squadrons, based on the horrific Triple-A they would have to face over Baghdad. These pilots would bring some of the 417th's aircraft over to be "attrition fillers!"

One of these pilots was Captain James R. Mastny (Bandit # 268). "We found out about the war starting in a roundabout way. Based in our quarters at Tonopah, we were notified not to go into work that day and the notice told us to stay in 'crew rest.'

Actually the reason for that was if we had done any flying, we would not have been considered rested enough to fly the aircraft over to Langley AFB. If we were ordered to fly the aircraft all the way to Saudi Arabia, they wanted to make sure we would be physically capable of it. After we found all of these notices that had been slid under our doors, we turned on CNN and lo ... the war had started. We had no idea until we turned on the television! Then it dawned on us as to why we were in crew rest.

Captain Scott Stimpert has just finished his tour out of Khamis (soon after the war ended) and he is ambushed by fellow pilot Major Jon Boyd in the hangar. Both of these pilots flew numerous missions all over Iraq. The aircraft shown here was showing 20 combat missions under the canopy rail. There were very few combat pilots in the Gulf War who faced the intensity of Triple-A that the F-117 pilots did. Excellent mission planning and a lot of luck got each of the aircraft through the "popcorn popper" over Baghdad. (Scott Stimpert)

"We were told to ferry eight F-117s over to Langley. Six of these aircraft were from the 417th Squadron and the other two had been left behind by one of the other squadrons due to maintenance problems. Our purpose was to fill the gaps left by the aircraft that were shot down over Iraq. By the third or fourth day of the war, it was obvious that the losses, if any, were going to be minimal! We sat at Langley for eight days before we were cleared to fly over to Khamis. We launched at about 12:30 P.M. on 25 January, accompanied by KC-135 tankers. The long flight was brutal! You try sitting in a stiff-back dining room chair for 14 hours and don't move except to push your legs forward to stretch them. We had two box lunches and all portions were cut into small sections to make it easier to consume, with all our bulky flight gear on.

"The sun came up over the Mediterranean when we were close to Egypt. At this time, we were so tired that some of the guys were dozing off, so we started talking to one another to stay awake! We still had one final refueling to go. The sun was right in our eyes as the tanker was flying due east. At this time, we were close to twelve hours into the flight. As we left our tankers, we had to fly into Saudi Arabia via the Red Sea as we could not fly over Egypt. We were given a frequency to contact the Saudi controllers on, so Tim Phillips, who was leading the entire package tried to make contact and nobody answered! He tried again and still no answer. Prior to this, we had to contact an aircraft carrier that was on station in the Red Sea, so they wouldn't scramble on us. We had a code word to say to them and they knew we were coming. Once we had given the password, we were clear to move through the airspace they were protecting, which was the Western flank. This confirmed that our radios were working. Finally, we were about to coast in over Saudi airspace and a controller comes on. He asked us who we were and we gave him our call sign. He was not going to let us in, so Tim tells him that we were going in if it meant stealthing up to do it. After what seemed like a longer period than it actually was, we landed at Khamis Mushait on 26 January at 10:00 in the morning." Now, the 37th Wing was bolstered by an additional eight aircraft and pilots, so there would be even more F-117s placed into the mission rotation, which was not good news for the Iraqi war effort.

The early presence of the 417th in the war is further explained by the squadron's commanding officer, Lt. Colonel Robert Maher (Bandit #308). "We arrived in theatre on Day-10 of the war and were soon integrated into the operational units. The 417th did not exist as a squadron during the war and my guys were generally distributed to the operational squadrons that they had come from originally. I was made an ADO (Assistant Director of Operations) under Colonel Klaus Klause. I spent most of my time in the command post or supervising the combat mission planners or mission briefings ... not that any of them needed help from me! The pilots flew every other day on the average and spent the off day mission planning. Like Colonels Whitley and Klause, I flew every third day, so that there were always two of us on the ground and available at any given time. I had flown a total of ten sorties by the time the war ended. When I landed after my tenth, I was greeted by Lt. Colonel Gonyea and a large water hose! That is when I learned my brief combat stint had come to an end and I would be going back to the states to get the training program restarted." While the 417th pilots had not logged any time during the Desert Shield work ups, their training regimen back at Tonopah insured that they would blend in with the others, perfectly. At this point, the complement of aircraft and pilots was at its maximum for the duration of the Gulf War.

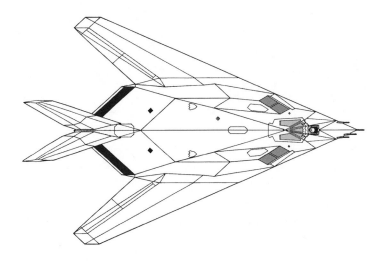

Captain James R. Mastny relaxes in the cockpit of the F-117 he will fly over Iraq, later that night. On most nights, the aircraft flew twice. There was no set pattern as to which aircraft each pilot flew. This was taken inside one of the hardened-aircraft shelters at Khamis. The Stealth is capable of carrying 4000 pounds of precision-guided bombs over a long distance and delivering them with unrivaled accuracy—at night. The F-117 is much bigger than it appears in pictures. (Scott Stimpert)

Chapter Four

Stealth Pilots Attack

The risk factor was not limited to just Iraqi airspace as far as the F-117 pilots were concerned. There were a few problems that cropped up either en route to the border or on the return. At least two pilots reported that they had engines catch on fire while they were hooked up to the tankers. This could have been a disastrous situation, but the calm reaction by the pilots made it just another tense day at the office. Both Major George Kelman and Captain Marcel Kerdavid encountered this problem. Both of the incidents were caused by a faulty seal around the receptacle. Kerdavid disconnected from the tanker and landed at the nearest base which was Taif.

Major Kelman remembers this incident in detail. "One night, heading in toward Iraq, we had been having trouble with fuel spray off the refueling probe leaking back along the top of the aircraft that was being refueled, causing a fire. I had a fuel manifold that connects the aerial refueling manifold into the aircraft. It seems that a few of the nuts that secure this apparatus had backed off, become loose, and it was letting some of the leaking fuel inside my aircraft. It was spraying it back over my #1 engine. At the time, I was on the boom of the tanker and I heard this calm voice say, 'You're on fire!' At the time I was thinking to myself, this was the last top off before hitting the border and I was totally focused on the details of the mission ahead. I said to myself, 'How stupid!!' You should always use call signs. It didn't sound like it had come from the intercom. So I'm thinking someone is on fire and they don't even know it! Then I hear the same transmission again ... same voice ... 'Hey! You're on fire.' These guys are out of their minds! He should be using call signs! All of a sudden, the boom operator disconnects and I look down at my

This seasoned group of people made up the mission planning cell at Khamis right after the war ended. The F-117s kept a major presence in the area for quite some time as a precaution. These planners were ready to plan strikes immediately, if the need had come up. In the center (front) is Major K. D. Boyer, one of the Electronic Warfare officers who had experience throughout Desert Storm while working in the planning cell for the Stealth squadrons. (Keith Boyer)

fuel gauge and I immediately see that I'm not full yet! Again this voice says, 'You're on fire.' That got my attention and I say, 'Hey! Are you talking to me?' About that time, my fire light comes on 'Holy Sh__! I am on fire!'

"It was the right engine. I pulled the throttle back and as a result of immediate reflexes brought on by the training I had received, I checked the clock. I looked around the cockpit and all I could see was that bright red light. I was going to wait fifteen seconds before doing anything. At that time, I stop-cocked the engine (cut off fuel flow) and shut it off ... hit the fire button and was going to count to ten, then hit the agent (fire retardant) and by the time the count reached three, the light went out. I can tell you it was a big relief! Here I was going in with two bombs and only one engine. I told my wingman to carry on and I contacted the AWACS, explaining the problem and told them I was diverting to the closest emergency base (using the code name), which was actually Al Kharj Air Base. I started heading over there and it was a distance of about 240 miles from my current location.

"I got down to a certain altitude where I could fly single engine. We kept some of our maintenance personnel based at this particular location, just for something like this. They were waiting

Major K.D. Boyer on the right gives a briefing on the post war Stealth capabilities to President George Bush and Secretary of the Air Force Rice at an open house. This was soon after the Gulf War, and any presentations on the F-117 were extremely popular with the media and government officials. Major Boyer was the key EWO in the Stealth Mission Planning Cell, during Desert Storm. Most of his flying time had been done in the back seat of the F4G Wild Weasel. (K.D. Boyer)

for me when I taxied up. About two and a half hours later, with all the panels removed, they had the problem identified, got it fixed, started up the engine and there were no leaks. I was ready to go. Calling for a release, I was told to wait until the next afternoon to bring my aircraft back to Khamis. I argued for a few seconds and they told me to stay put. Well, here I was bunking about 300 yards from the runway and the base was running around-the-clock operations with their F-15Cs. They were taking off in full afterburner and I got no sleep! The next day, I got back to our base with no problems, caught up on my rest, and worked back into the rotation."

Many hours were spent by the planners in fine tuning the missions. These pilots are going over some last-minute details of an upcoming strike against targets in Baghdad. Left to right: John "Pete" Peterson, Terry Foley, Rich Treadway, and 416th Squadron Commander Greg Gonyea. At the far left, the heart-shaped figure with the handprints on it was a special project from an elementary school classroom back in the states. (Scott Stimpert)

This was taken right after Night One of the war. These pilots were going over the details of their first night's missions and getting ready for their next target assignments over Iraq. Left to right: Greg Gonyea (416th C.O.), John Savidge, Scott Stimpert, Rich Treadway, and Rod Shrader. These five pilots flew combat in the war from Night One and they went up against just about every type of target with which the Wing was tasked. (Scott Stimpert)

While the buildup was underway in Desert Shield, the Iraqi Air Force was flexing its muscles across the border and every movement was being monitored by Coalition Intelligence from Saudi airspace. Based on figures compiled at the time, the Iraqis were accumulating about 100 sorties (of all types) per day. Their inventory of aircraft was impressive and it had held a dominating edge over the Iranians during their long war. But, once the Gulf War started, the Iraqi Air Force dwindled down to only a token threat within four days. When the F-117s made their first forays over Baghdad, they encountered several MiGs that were flying CAPs (Combat Air Patrol) over the city, but the Iraqi pilots never knew they were there.

A few of the Stealth pilots related their experiences involving MiG encounters while on their "downtown" missions. One of those pilots was Major Joe Bouley who was paired up with

Opening night of the Gulf War. These 416th pilots have finished their briefings and are ready to fly their F-117s into harm's way. Standing is Jerry Sink. Left to right: Rich Treadway, Mike Mahar, Terry Foley, Rich Cline, Phil McDaniel, John Savidge, and Rod Shrader. This was taken in the Operations Room, 16 January 1991. (Scott Stimpert)

Lt. Colonel Barry Horne, flying on the second night of the war. While the F-117 usually flew against targets as singles, on this mission they would both be going after the same target. Their strike plan called for a spacing between the aircraft of one minute.

Bouley recalls, "We had topped off from the tanker and were about 60 miles inside Iraq. I don't know if Lt. Colonel Horne saw them or not, but I spotted two MiG-23s with my infrared. They were heading west, in formation. More than likely they were on a CAP, but evidently they were never aware that either of us were anywhere around. We continued on to the west and then moved over to the northwest corner of Baghdad before we turned in to the target. The city was lit up from one end to the other and an occasional SAM was being fired straight up. My eyes were focused on my infrared and I could see several aircraft flying around on the perimeter of the city, but they were too far off to tell if they were ours or theirs. I'm sure if they were Iraqi, that they were staying clear of all the Triple-A that was being thrown up."

In checking the final statistics from the Gulf War, the tally sheet shows that there were a total of five MiG-29s and eight MiG-23s shot down. It was the latter that were owned in the largest numbers by the Iraqi Air Force. Most of the nocturnal encounters that were recalled by the Stealth pilots were of MiG-23s over the general vicinity of Baghdad. Major George Kelman said he flew through the middle of a MiG CAP, completely unnoticed. "On my first mission which was on the night of 17 January, I was going

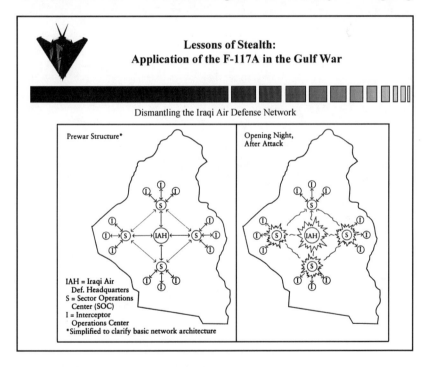

These two diagrams show exactly what the F-117 and TLAMs were tasked with accomplishing on the first night of the war. On the left are the integrated air defense systems that made Iraq one of the most hostile and dangerous air spaces in the world. The right diagram shows how all of the air defense capabilities were mostly destroyed that first night, by precision strikes carried out by the Stealth. (Rod Shrader)

downtown to knock out the National Computer Center along with a hardened command center around Al Taqaddum (on the west side of Baghdad). I proceeded around to the east side of the city which had a slight cloud layer over it. I saw two MiG-23s coming straight at me from the opposite direction ... probably at a distance of ten miles away, but it seemed much closer to me. I moved my infrared over that way and took a look at them. They were easily spotted because they had their lights on. None of the friendlies would have been flying in that area with their lights on! I believe I was in the middle of a routine night patrol. They came right by me and continued off in the opposite direction and they never turned back my way. I do remember that my heart rate went up during those brief seconds."

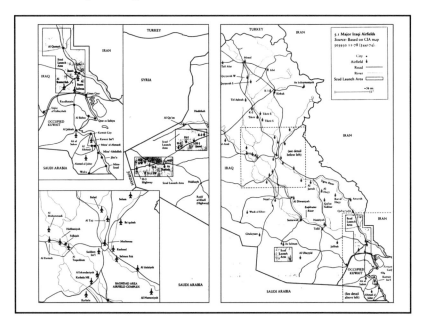

These maps show the excessive number of airfields that had been built in Iraq since the late 1960s. About the time that the tensions were mounting between Iran and Iraq, the CIA outlined the locations of these key air bases (1978). By the time Desert Shield was initiated, these were the most up-to-date maps of Iraq's air assets. As the Coalition forces gathered in Saudi Arabia, their Intel quickly brought the Iraqi military strengths into focus. (Rod Shrader)

On at least one occasion, the F-117 came face to face with the Soviet made MiG-29. From all indications the stealth technology was working perfectly on every encounter with the Iraqi fighters at night. They had their airborne intercept radar working, but any guidance from their controllers was suspect, because their radar and communications had been all but destroyed. None of the enemy pilots were ever aware that the F-117s were close enough to see them, but they certainly knew that it wasn't just the TLAMs that were taking out all of their key assets. Major Wes Wyrick was the pilot who mentioned he had flown in close to some MiG-29s when he was approaching his first target of the night. "This mission was during the first few days of the war and the Iraqis were still putting up some fighters at night to fly the

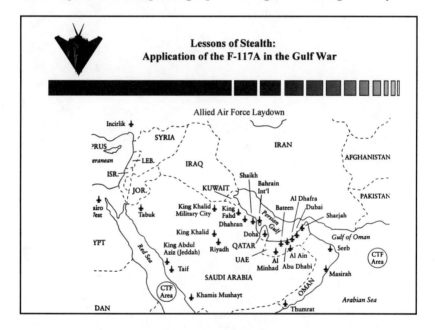

By early January 1991, the Coalition forces had established a well-protected ring of air bases all over Saudi Arabia. Scattered around in the forward areas were the F-15C which was the most lethal air-to-air predator in the arsenal. The bases located furthest from the Iraqi border were used by the F-117s, B-52s, and the F-111s. These were the heavy-duty strikers and they could operate safely out of the Scud missile range. The Stealth unit was based out of Khamis, in the lower left of the map. (Rod Shrader)

barrier patrols. I can remember coming in right under a couple of orbiting MiG-29s that never had a clue I was around. My target was acquired and hit successfully and I egressed out of the area without any problems from them." After the war ended, one of the forward air controllers for the 82nd Airborne Division was assigned the task of observing the damage done to a few of the major Iraqi airfields. He stated that when he went into a bombed-out Iraqi operations building, on the bulletin board was a crude drawing of the silhouette of an F-117 and a B-2. This proved that their pilots were indeed aware of what might have been flying over Iraqi airspace at night.

The faceting around the canopy and FLIR turret is evident in this photo. The FLIR turret is turned in toward the aircraft — its normal position to protect the optics. Only when it is being used does the turret face forward, exposing the IR sensor and laser designator. (Lockheed Martin Skunk Works/Eric Schulzinger)

There was always the possibility of an Iraqi night fighter just probing around in the dark, hoping to encounter a Nighthawk by sheer luck. After Day 4 of the war, the chances of this happening were dim, because most if not all of the MiGs had been shot down or were hidden away in aircraft shelters hoping to survive the war. Still, this was not a proven fact. Some F-117 pilots recall being startled by the reflection of cockpit lights at a very close range and after a couple of tense seconds, they realized it was the other half of their two-ship and not a MiG. On one mission early on, Major Jon "Jonboy" Boyd and Major Charles "T-Pup" Treadway were a two-ship on a mission into Iraq. Treadway

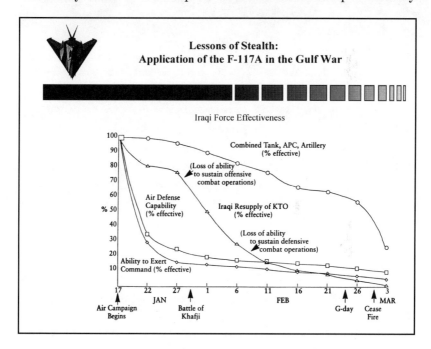

The battle plan that was engineered by General Norman Schwarzkopf and his staff was carried out to perfection. This illustration shows that during the first few nights of the war, the Iraqi's ability to command and control their assets out in the field, had all but been taken away. The items shown here, that had the least priority, were the tanks and artillery. As the time came closer for the ground war to begin, the F-15Es and A-10s went after these and as shown here, with devastating results. (Rod Shrader)

The Stealth organization had a heavy work schedule during its involvement in Desert Storm. The maintenance troops worked all day long and into the night, until the third and final wave of F-117s was launched against Iraq. The pilots flew long hours during the night and briefed late in the afternoon. It was this around-the-clock effort that made the performance record of the Wing one of the best in military aviation history. (Rose Reynolds)

recalls that night. "Always aware of the threat of bad guys flying around looking to find us, I used to spend a good bit of time looking into the darkness for the enemy, particularly on egress after the bombs were away and I didn't have much else to think about. On one particular night, I was aware that one of my squadron mates, "Jonboy" Boyd was going to be in very close proximity to me, but I wasn't exactly sure of how close. While cruising home after my targets had been hit, I was preoccupied with a small system problem and just happened to look up and around for a quick visual search. There, looming behind me, was a shadowy shape, barely discernible in the darkness!! My heart jumped. I considered a dozen options for defense, weighed them as best I could, and came up with a plan. I selected the appropriate frequency, forcefully pushed the transmit button, and declared as clearly as I could, 'Oh, Jonboy, I hope that's you!!' The answer was affirmative! What a relief!"

From the other half of that two-ship, Major Boyd tells his view of the same mission. "Our INS (Inertial Navigational System) was so good that we would fly with an altitude split of only a very short distance, flying just a few seconds off lead's time and you would be in formation, so to speak, even if it was total darkness outside and you couldn't see each other. We noticed this especially when

The F-117's impressive record of achievements that continued to mount as the war progressed, caught the eye of all the top-ranking officers from the coalition. On this occasion, two top-ranking officers from the Saudi Air Force pay a visit to the 37th Wing's base at Khamis Mushait. On the far right is Lt. General Charles Horner, Joint Force Component Commander and on the left (partially hidden) is Colonel Al Whitley, 37th Wing Commander. The Stealth's ability to hit any target in Baghdad, at will, held a fascination for all of the ranking officers involved in the war. (Rose Reynolds)

The ordnance crews were kept busy most of the day and into the night, until the third wave of strikers had been loaded out. The Mission Planning Cell determined what type of bombs would be used against each target. On a large number of the missions, the F-117s were carrying two different types of bombs and each one was earmarked for a specific target. All four of these shown here were GBUs weighing 2,000 pounds each. When the larger bombs became scarce in number, they utilized 500 pounders against targets that the smaller bombs would be effective against. (Rose Reynolds)

This picture was taken inside a damaged hardened aircraft shelter after the war ended. Everything under its roof was reduced to rubble. The steel reinforcing rods were twisted like pretzels. Major Rob Donaldson poses underneath the massive hole in the roof. On the newer Iraqi shelters, the GBU-10s did not have the punch to destroy them, so the weapon of choice was the GBU-27. (Rob Donaldson)

Ordnance Specialists from the 37th Wing perform last-minute inspections of laser-guided bombs prior to the night's mission. (Rose Reynolds)

The patches that follow all pertain to the F-117 program, ranging from its inception at Lockheed Skunk Works through Operation Desert Storm.

Early on in the Gulf War, the need to service F-117s increased to the point of supporting three full strikes against Iraq, per night. This meant that the aircraft in the first wave were serviced and reloaded in preparation for flying the third and final attack. In most cases, the fighters who were involved in the last wave did not return to Khamis until after the sun had come up, as shown in this picture. (Rose Reynolds)

Although this was taken after the war had ended, the Stealth kept a presence in the Gulf region as a precaution against Iraq's saber rattling. A significant number of 416th FS aircraft and personnel remained at Khamis with a battle plan that could have been initiated within hours of any trouble. With the unrest and problems that the Coalition Forces had with the Iraqi leadership those months after the war, the Stealth aircraft could have been the first response to any aggressive action against Kuwait or any other friendly Arab country. (Marvin Lynchard)

Ordnance personnel watch one of their own taxi by en route to its take-off position. Both of these F-117s were probably slated for the first mission of the night, which usually launched right before dark. By the time they had traveled the 2.5 hour flight to the Iraqi border, it was totally dark. It was a tight squeeze to put up three strikes per night, but it was done by the 37th Wing on a regular basis. The hardened-aircraft shelters at Khamis Mushait were state-of-the-art and rated as some of the safest in the world. (Rose Reynolds)

This fully-loaded F-117, Mean Mist, *is waiting for the precise time to taxi for the night's mission. As seen in the markings near the canopy,* Mean Mist *had already flown 22 missions when this photo was taken.* (Rose Reynolds)

This picture is a good example of the damage that the GBU-10 could do with a dead center hit from an F-117. Everything that had been stored in this hardened shelter would have been burned to the ground, including any aircraft that had been parked in it. Some of the thicker-walled shelters had to be taken out by the GBU-27 bomb. At one point, the Iraqis were painting dark areas on the top of some shelters, so they would appear to have already been knocked out. At night, it was very difficult to tell the difference. (Guy Aceto / Air Force Association)

Above: Saudi Arabian patch for the stealth fighter base at Khamis Mushait.

we were coming back out from the target and were supposed to rendezvous to go to the tanker. You usually shared several points on your route prior to the join up and you'd start getting the timing set up. Soon, you could get the sh_t scared out of you when you noticed another aircraft nearby paralleling your course ... and it would be your wingman! I did that one night to 'T-Pup' and when I got to the switch on line, I heard him asking if it was me. Two mike clicks calmed us all down quickly! I don't believe that any of the MiGs stumbled onto us during those early days because the F-15s knocked most of them down early on."

A lone F-117 launches from Khamis Mushait for a test flight after maintenance. These subsonic fighters were capable of carrying two 2,000-pound "smart bombs" and deliver them with precision on any target in Iraq. Very seldom were both bombs dropped at the same time as each pilot usually had two targets assigned and after dropping the first one, it may have been another fifteen minutes or more before he was lining up his second and final bomb. (Rose Reynolds)

While the F-117s were free to roam the night skies over Iraq, they were, by no means, alone. It is true that the Iraqi MiGs were history by Day 4, but that left the ultimate nocturnal, air superiority predator, the F-15C Eagle. There were three Wings of these Eagles that were patrolling every night. Iraq was split into three lanes—East, Center, and West—and each was covered by one of the Eagle units. They would maintain a constant vigil from up on their perch. They would fly with external lights out and cockpit lights out with the exception of the map light on the fuel gauge. Needless to say, their night vision was uncanny as they could detect movement on the ground with the naked eye. On occasion,

Mission weary 415th Squadron pilot, Captain Rob Donaldson (center) manages a smile after a very long mission over Baghdad. His ground crew was waiting for him when he climbed out of his Stealth. Donaldson was in the first wave of F-117s (415th Squadron) to attack Iraq on that first night of the war. Their objective on that first night was to blind the Iraqi defenses so that they would not be able to detect the non-stealthy aircraft that would be coming into enemy airspace right after the first Stealth strike. (Rose Reynolds)

In the safety and shade of a hardened hangar, these support crews load the big GBU-27 bombs into the bay of a Stealth fighter. These were the most destructive bombs that were carried by the F-117 and they had deep-penetrating ability. Basically, they were used against tall buildings where the bombs had to go down several stories before detonating or they were effective against heavily fortified bunkers. There was no external ordnance carried by the Stealth for obvious reasons. (Rose Reynolds)

the stealthy movement of the F-117 in and out of Iraq was visually detected by the F-15 pilots although nothing registered on the radar scope. The input from one of the Eagle drivers will add credibility to the statements of the Stealth pilots as they looked out of their cockpits for any signs of other aircraft.

Captain Jay Denney, an F-15 pilot with the 36th Fighter Wing, comments on some of the things that he saw during those long night CAPs over Iraq. Denney was credited with shooting down two MiG-23s during the Gulf War. "We were responsible for capping in the Central Lane over Iraq. I was usually working an area that was about 75 miles south of Baghdad. From our altitude, it was easy to see the Triple-A, SAM launches, and bomb explosions within the city. We were over open desert and could see the roads, villages, encampments, some vehicle movement, etc.

The fatigue on this unidentified F-117 pilot shows as he pulls into his parking spot right outside the hardened shelters at Khamis. The average missions lasted from 5.5 hours to 8 hours depending on what part of Iraq their targets were located in. The missions up on the Turkish border lasted at least 8 hours and some Stealths were not yet into Saudi airspace when the sun came up. However, this area was well protected by large numbers of F-15 Eagles that were patrolling these corridors and there were no Iraqi fighters in this area after the first few days of the war. (Rose Reynolds)

From the FRAG/ATO we knew when the strikers, including the F-117s, would be at their tanker tracks, so from that you had a rough hack (knew the time) of when the ingress's were. Obviously, they went 'communications-out' once they pushed (crossed into enemy airspace), but they had a sanctuary altitude, just as EF-111s and EA-6Bs did to insure no one ran into them. The Eagles were always blocked high and while watching the ground action several times, we saw the F-117s fly underneath us, highlighted by a full moon and a relatively light desert background. After getting a visual on the first one, we began to look for them a little harder. Had we not known their altitude and actively searched for them (out of boredom), I don't think we would have seen as many as we did."

If there was one thing that the Stealth pilot feared it was being seen by an enemy gunner or aircraft, visually. It was taken for granted that in most cases, the chances of their being seen by radar were minimal. However, it would have been potentially fatal to stand out on a light background with a full moon out. Inclement weather was considered an asset except where it was blocking out the targets and reducing the chances of delivering an accurate bomb drop. Had the Coalition air forces not established air superiority early on, that F-15 could have been a MiG-23. More than one Stealth pilot commented that to be caught on top of cloud cover with a full moon above was like

The new hardened-aircraft shelters at Khamis Mushait had been built to accommodate the Saudi F-15s. The 37th Wing was able to house at least two Stealths per shelter. All of the service work, refueling, loading bombs, etc. was done within this covered area. When it came time to taxi out, the first aircraft in line was towed out before starting engines and the one behind rolled out of the shelter on its own power. This ship is being refueled for the mission that is still a few hours away. (Rose Reynolds)

being a roach running around on a white bed sheet! It was this fact that explained why weather on the night routes was discussed in detail at all the briefings at Khamis Mushait!

During the "43 Day War," the F-117 flew almost 1300 sorties against a wide variety of targets in Iraq and Kuwait, most of which were heavily defended. If one were to read a detailed account of each mission flown by each pilot, there would be a lot of repetition because all were very similar except for about two

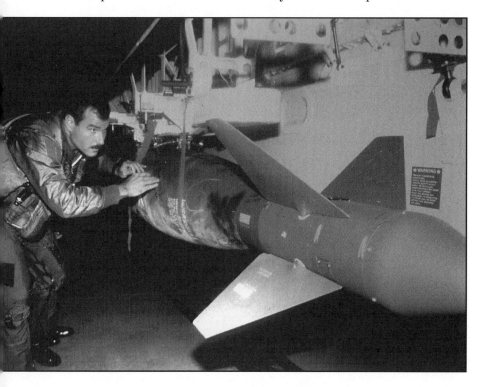

The 2,000-pound precision-guided bombs that the Stealth carried were capable of taking out just about any target in Iraq. For the deep bunkers or hardened-aircraft shelters (HAS), the GBU-27 was very effective. The GBU-10s were used most effectively against bridges and older aircraft hangars. Here, Captain Rob Donaldson carefully inspects one of the bombs that he will take into Iraq later that night. Being one of the original cadre of F-117 pilots to deploy to Saudi Arabia, Donaldson flew every night for the first few nights of the war. (Rob Donaldson)

Captain Wesley Cockman, a seasoned Stealth pilot, visits with some of the support personnel at Khamis. They are inside one of the heavily-fortified aircraft shelters that had just been built for the new Saudi F-15s. Adverse weather was never a factor with the maintenance crews working in these facilities. Captain Cockman completed his tour in the F-117 with 450 hours in the aircraft and 2800 total flying hours. The experience level of the Stealth pilots right before the Gulf air war started was very high. This was reflected in their record-breaking performance in combat. (Rose Reynolds)

minutes of every mission. It was during these brief "bomb runs" that each sortie developed its own personality. On an average, each pilot probably remembers only one or two missions vividly and the rest seem to blend into one. In questioning a number of pilots about missions where some of the more spectacular secondary explosions occurred, most will name the one flown by Lt. Colonel Barry Horne, Operations Officer for the 415th Squadron. Not only was it impressive to the pilot who dropped the bomb, but to all of the F-117 pilots who were in trail or even the ones ahead of him. It was flown after the war was several days old.

Lt. Colonel Horne states, "This particular mission was a two-target one and the ammunition bunker was Target #1. My secondary target for the night was a chemical storage bunker. The ammo dump was in the west central part of Iraq (approximately 100 miles west of Baghdad). Target #2 was just slightly north of Baghdad. The mission was flown at a medium altitude and the munition selected to use on it was the deep penetrating GBU-27. The target lay in a vast array of uniformly-placed bunkers in a very flat, open area. Other bunkers had been hit before, but many of them still remained intact. This bunker was actually a

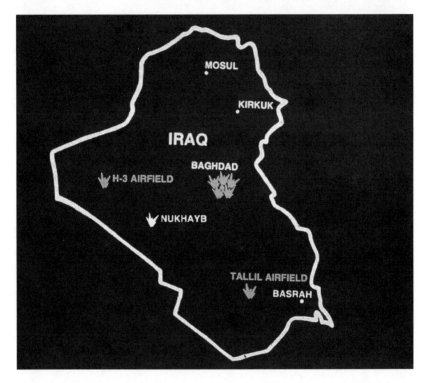

This map of Iraq was used in numerous briefings after Desert Storm. It shows the location of the major targets located within its boundaries. Kuwait was located at the lower portion below Iraq. Even though there were several key targets in Kuwait, this map only shows the aggressor country. Up at the top is Mosul, which housed many major targets that had to be attacked by the F-117, due to the heavy Triple-A and SAM cover around the area. The length of these missions consistently lasted longer than seven hours and called for the tankers to follow the "black jets" into Iraq for a limited distance to insure that they had enough fuel to make it back out again. (Rob Donaldson)

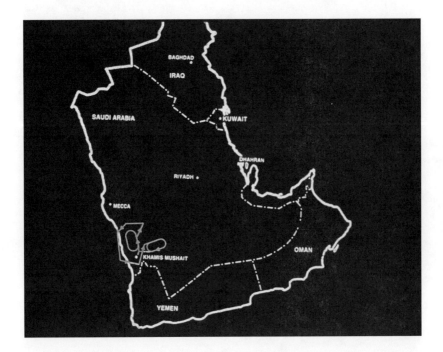

In the lower left portion of this map of Saudi Arabia is Khamis Mushait, the sole operating base assigned to the Stealth during Desert Shield and Storm. It was tucked away at a great distance from Iraq and for reason. During the war, it was out of range for the notorious "Scud" missiles. The only danger of attack at the base, was from Yemen, a short distance to the south. Saudi F-15s did a barrier CAP against such attacks. (Rob Donaldson)

double bunker configuration. I approached the target from south to north, and perpendicular to its layout. I used only one bomb and after release, I detected that the thumb tracker was overly sensitive, which caused me considerable difficulty late in the maneuver!

"At one point, the tracker caused the sightline to move, or rather jump approximately 100 feet south of the target. I did regain control and managed to steer the weapon to final impact. The bomb hit precisely in the middle of the bunker, at the wall that separated the two bunkers. The explosion was brilliant, seem-

The F-117 shown here has already logged 22 combat missions over Iraq and Kuwait. It would be difficult to determine at what point it was in the war by looking at the mission hacks, because some of the aircraft flew twice in one night. There were a few F-117s that ended up with close to 40 missions before the war ended. The in-service rate remained extremely high due to the maintenance people's hard work and long hours. There were only a few maintenance problems that cropped up which couldn't be fixed in a matter of hours. (Rose Reynolds)

ingly engulfing, not only underneath me, but also it seemed to engulf the sky all around me. For a brief moment, I was afraid that it might frag me or even reach up and grab me. I continued on to my next target north of Baghdad. That bomb hit the target with no problem and as I egressed from the target area to the border, I looked back to the west and even though it had been over twenty minutes since I hit the ammo bunker, there was a huge hot glow in the distance! The intelligence people and munitions experts, who viewed the tapes, said it was the largest explosion they had ever viewed! One told me that there was probably over a million pounds of explosives stored in the two bunkers. I didn't fly over that area again, but it must have left an impressive crater!"

The F-117 pilot who had been flying about fifty miles ahead of Lt. Colonel Horne on this mission was Captain Rob Donaldson. He can still picture the explosion in his mind. "I had just hit my targets for the night and was in the process of turning around to head back. All of a sudden, with total darkness all around me, there was this explosion behind me and in a matter of two seconds, the entire sky lit up. I looked back behind me and it would be difficult to find the words to perfectly describe what I saw. It appeared to be a nuclear blast close to Baghdad and I knew that Horne was behind me and he was probably caught up in it! The explosion created a mushroom cloud and a massive fireball. All of my antennae had been retracted into the aircraft, which meant I could not communicate with anyone or find out what it was. At that point, I turned on my tape recorder to record what I had just seen along with the exact time and location. The shock wave from the blast rocked my aircraft as I moved back through the area. At one point, it was like daylight outside of the cockpit. After returning to base, I found out that it had been a well-placed GBU-27 that had done the damage and not a nuke."

Observed from another angle and point of view, Major Leatherman adds his comments on that mission. "As far as spectacular explosions from a bomb hit, you know that Iraq was like one big ammo dump! I didn't have any secondary blasts like the one that Barry Horne got. Our Intelligence was constantly picking up info about new ones and we would be tasked to hit them. I can remember a mission where I was over Baghdad and I knew that a couple of our guys were going after these new dumps at about the same time. It happened to be just south of where I had finished off my last target and I knew the TOT (time over target) for the other two which was just seconds after mine. I remember turning out of there and actually seeing the explosion from one of these bunkers going up and that turned out to be the one that Horne got. I mean you could see it from 50-60 miles away and it looked like a small nuclear explosion. Back then, our humor was kind of black and I can remember sitting up there smiling, thinking that somebody must have found something big!! After we had all landed, I can remember everyone gathered around to watch

An ordnance specialist makes final adjustments to one of the 2,000-pound bombs that have been loaded into an F-117's twin bays. Pilots flew the majority of their missions with one of two bombs: the GBU-10 and the GBU-27, both of which weighed the same. When striking the newer aircraft shelters, the Stealth pilots reported that their GBU-10s bounced off like tennis balls. They came back the next night with the deep penetrating GBU-27s and destroyed everything within these shelters. (Rose Reynolds)

the video of Barry's impressive hit. The explosion engulfed his entire screen in a massive fireball."

Not all of the memorable fireballs brought on by well-placed ordnance were from secondary explosions. Captain Jim Mastny of the 417th Squadron remembers one such mission that left a distinct impression with him. "I do remember one night I was flying on a mission, eastbound towards a radio facility in Kuwait City, kind of down in the southeast corner of Iraq. Our Coalition forces were known to use some of those big 'daisy cutters' from the Vietnam era. They were huge bombs that were rolled out of the back of C-130s. (These were the BLU-82s that weighed 15,000 pounds. They were delivered out of the back of MC-130Es).

A lone F-117 taxies back to its hardened-aircraft shelter after returning from the last mission of the night. The third and final wave of Stealths usually found it difficult to make it back out of Iraqi airspace before sunrise. They were usually very low on fuel by the time they reached the Saudi border and after topping off their tanks, they still had a 2.5 hour flight back to Khamis. Many pilots recalled how relaxed they were as they enjoyed the sunrises over friendly airspace and played favorite sound tracks on their Sony Walkmans. Quite a come-down from two or three hours previously when they were flying through a wall of hot lead over Baghdad. (Rose Reynolds)

I believe they were used back then to make instant clearings in the jungle for helicopters to land. During this period in the Gulf War, they were dropping some of these on targets associated with Iraq's Republican Guard. On top of this, our B-52s were pounding the Guard around the clock. I think it was meant to prevent these forces from getting any needed sleep. Anyway, I'm flying eastbound on a target with the second 'go' of the night and it's pitch black out there. I was looking out of the cockpit as we often did, when you could see the bomb blasts from one of our aircraft off in the distance. This would usually be followed by a heavy barrage of Triple-A ... all in the distance.

"From where I was, you had a good view of all the areas that were under attack by the F-117s. All of a sudden, night turns into day up here in my cockpit. It is extremely bright. I looked around and couldn't see what had happened. The blast turned the sky orange for a few seconds. I quickly wrote down my position from the reading on my INS. This would allow me to give accurate info to our Intel people and they could use it to determine what happened, if they didn't already know. Did someone shoot a SAM at me? I had never seen anything like it before. When I got back on the ground, I reported to them and I was told that they were dropping the big bombs on the Guard positions. They told me that it had detonated just as I cleared over it. They had the time deconflicted so I wouldn't be right over it. Very impressive explosion!"

Chapter Five

Attacking Iraq's Heavily-Defended Airfields

M ost of the Iraqi airfield complexes were scattered out over a wide area, away from Baghdad. At the beginning of the Gulf Air war, these bases were jammed with aircraft and there had been very little effort to shield or disperse these assets away from the potential might of the Coalition forces. Part of this mind-set of the Iraqis might have been brought on by the fact that Iran had not been able to penetrate their defenses and bomb their aircraft. Nevertheless, the larger airfields were very heavily defended by Triple-A and SAMs. The intensity of this fire-power proved to be a dangerous liability for the F-117s.

Wing Commander Whitley talks about these memorable missions he flew over the same complex, the Balad Southeast airfield which was 40 miles north of the city. Their ordnance did not produce the results that they were supposed to. "Early in the conflict, we were directed against a large number of hardened-aircraft shelters (HAS) with a substantial force of F-117s. Unfortunately, we had the wrong weapons on board. We were tasked to go against these targets with 2,000 pound blast-fragmentation bombs with a nose plug and delayed tail fuse. Although we vehemently objected to the CENTAF planning staff on the weapons selection, but were told to salute and execute, so we did! The results were pitiful against this very heavily defended target.

"While the weapons folks built and loaded the bombs as directed, while the supply, support, maintenance, and Intel people did their standard exemplary job of supporting this mission, the results were miserable despite outstanding accuracy on the part of our pilots. In almost every case, the bombs simply exploded on the exterior of the shelters, causing little damage to the struc-

In the months that followed the Stealth's return from the war, it was the most sought after aircraft for all the air shows and open houses. Captain Rob Donaldson was lucky enough to be able to fly his F-117 up to the big Oshkosh Event in 1991. He was also able to have his wife, Millie, attend. Both of them pose for the camera in front of the Stealth display amidst a near record turnout for the event. (Rob Donaldson)

ture or their contents. While the explosions made for some very impressive video, the pilots were not too happy about being exposed to such stiff ground defenses for so little in terms of results. We learned a valuable lesson from this incident, and subsequently fought other battles with the planning staff to ensure our weapons system was being employed in the most appropriate manner. Bomb selection or this target had nothing to do with a lack of understanding for the F-117. It was a breakdown in 'the system' which led to a waste of some very valuable combat sorties."

Rob Donaldson, 415th Squadron pilot, elaborates on the missions mentioned above. "To give you an example of the two types of ordnance we carried, one night ten of us took off and went against the big airfield known as Balad Southeast. Our Intelligence had it that Hussein had packed a large number of fighters into some of his newer aircraft shelters at this airfield. We were all loaded with GBU-10s which our mission planners, up at CENTAF, determined would do the job. These HAS were much tougher than they had anticipated because our bombs either exploded on the surface or just bounced off like tennis balls. We were amazed that there was little or no effect. This must have left a positive impression on the Iraq brass, because the next day, they began jamming all types of aircraft into these 'bomb proof' shelters. The next night we went back against these same HAS, only this time we were loaded with the big penetrators: the GBU-27s. They drove right through the layers of concrete and steel, exploding with a terrific force inside each shelter. The heavy steel doors on both ends were blown out and pieces of aircraft and debris came flying out. Everything that was on the inside was totally destroyed."

It is interesting to note that several of the pilots had comments about the ineffective, bouncing GBU-10s that had been sent against the heavily fortified aircraft shelters. Captain Michael Riehl (Bandit #320) gives us some excellent details on one of the missions he helped plan and also participated in. "One of the missions that I remember the best was one that I helped plan

The Patriot air defense missile probably had more publicity and was more readily known among the people back home than the Tomahawk (TLAM) or the Stealth fighter. Of the eighty-six Scuds fired at Saudi Arabia and Israel by Iraq, thirty nine fell harmlessly into the desert. Of the forty seven that were headed for populated areas, the Patriots intercepted all but two. (K.D. Boyer)

against Balad Southeast Airfield. This particular mission falls into the category of 'I'd rather be lucky than good!!' Previously, the F-111Fs had tried to hit it and had been turned back due to extremely heavy Triple-A. We had been pounding other airfields with great success. Most of the revetments at other Iraqi airfields looked like A-frames with the top chopped off or some looked like Quonset huts made of concrete. When we got our Intel photos of the revetments, they were very broad and looked like they could hold a couple of aircraft side by side. They also had the look of something that was going to be very hard to crack!

"When I looked at the frag (bomb target orders) that had come down from Riyadh, they had assigned GBU-10s to the target. I went straight to our weapons officer and told him I thought we should use the GBU-27s, but he assured me that the -10s ought to be able to do the job. We made some minor adjustments to the nose of the bomb to make it a little more effective. The rest of the mission planning went as expected. Our aircraft were planned to hit a revetment with one of their bombs, do a timing loop and then hit another revetment before egressing out. To help negate the Triple-A, we planned our attack at a specific (classified) altitude.

"When we flew the mission, all started out well. Route navigation was relatively straight forward. They apparently were expecting a low altitude attack again because the ground fire started going off after the first bomb impacted. Most of it was

Major Jeff "Jammer" Moore poses with Darth Vader, who could easily be described as the pilot of the ominous looking black jet. This was taken at an Air Show after Desert Storm (El Paso, Texas). At this time, the F-117 was at its peak in popularity with Americans. The crowds gathered at these shows in such cities as El Paso, Memphis, Honolulu, Minot, and Oshkosh openly showed their appreciation for what their military had accomplished in the brief war over Iraq. (Jeff "Jammer" Moore)

fused well below our altitude. However, there was quite a bit of 57mm that was going off above our altitude. My first bomb was a no-guide, so I flew the timing loop and came back for the re-attack. I guided my second GBU-10 and it hit dead center, but instead of seeing a hole in the revetment and the ends blowing out as I was used to, all I got was a smoke ring!! You could actually see the entire revetment through the expanding smoke ring. It made me mad and I thought that I must have had a bad bomb. As it turned out, every one of our GBU-10s had done the same thing. It turned out, as I suspected in the mission planning that

On the right is Captain Jenni Whitnack, commanding officer of the Logistics Support Squadron at Tonopah Test Range and Stealth pilot, Captain John Hesterman. This was taken at Nellis AFB in December 1991, after the war. In April 1993, the couple was married. Both have continued their careers in the USAF. (Bernhard-Williams)

One of the most successful pen pal relationships to come out of the Gulf War is shown in this photograph. On the left is Sara Caldwell from Fayetteville, Arkansas and on the right is Major Joseph Bouley, an F-117 pilot in the 415th Squadron. They began to exchange letters on a regular basis during Desert Shield, however their friendship developed into more than just pen pals. This was taken right after Bouley returned to Las Vegas when the war ended. Sara flew out to meet him for the first time. After eight months of writing and six weeks of dating, they were married in Las Vegas with the entire 415th squadron in attendance. (Joe Bouley)

the revetments at Balad SE were too hard for the ordnance we had selected. It was a big disappointment to me to have been in on the planning of an entire squadron attack on the airfield and to have it turn out to be a dud because of my bad planning!

"Now, we get to the part where it is better to be lucky than good! Apparently, the Iraqis thought our failed attempt on the airfield was due to these revetments being of a superior design. They started flying all of their aircraft that they had left at other bases, to Balad SE. We learned this from our Intel sources in Riyadh. We were tasked to re-attack the airfield and this time we would be carrying GBU-27s! Now, we knew we had full revetments, instead of some of them being empty like in the previous attack. The deep penetrator GBU-27s made short work of the revetments just like they did with everything else. The result of the failed attack and re-attack was the fact that the Iraqi pilots began fleeing to Iran with their aircraft and our F-15 Eagles were chasing them down and popping all the ones that they could." It would be the 33rd Fighter Wing's F-15Cs, out of Eglin AFB that would end up with the most enemy aircraft destroyed.

It was against a variety of airfields over a three week period that the laser-guided smart bombs really earned their reputation, at least with the Stealth pilots. Many of these bombs that were dropped on the revetments/shelters had to be re-directed after they had already departed the aircraft. Captain John Hesterman (Bandit #339) relates a mission where he had the opportunity to destroy a MiG. "One of my most memorable flights into Iraq happened a little later on in the war. I flew in a two-ship with my operations officer, Lt. Colonel Barry Horne. We were ordered to go against some hardened-aircraft shelters at Al Asad Airfield. Not much activity had been reported at this base on previous strikes, so we went in expecting very little opposition. There were some clouds around as we approached the airfield, so we both had elected to fly at our minimum backup altitudes to give ourselves the best chance of seeing the target. The risk, of course, was that the back-up altitude would be within the range of the Triple-A that was positioned around this specific target.

"About a minute out from the drop, the airfield lit up like Christmas in New York City. They had apparently moved several of the guns in and around the base to protect the aircraft that had recently been moved there. We both hit our first targets and looped back around to run the gauntlet again. I can remember thinking, I hope he (Lt. Colonel Horne) didn't come down to this altitude and if he did, I hope he was smart enough not to try it again! It turned out we were both at low altitude and neither of us was smart enough not to go back in. I know many of us had decided early in the war, not to turn back from Triple-A fire. I figured we had the luxury of not being susceptible to the radar-guided fire that other aircrews in other aircraft types had to put up with, so we ought to be assets used against the heavily defended targets (not that my rationalization made it any more fun!). At least the F-117 made you keep your head down during the actual strike, so the elation of a direct hit usually lasted at least until you looked back outside and realized you didn't want to be there anymore.

"On the second pass at Al Asad, I could not see the target clearly when it was time to drop because of the smoky haze from our

Shortly after the Gulf War was over, a special display was set up for Congress at Andrews AFB. This was primarily made up of three aircraft: F-117, B-2, and F-22. It was not only attended by Congress, but also by President George Bush and several government VIPs. This picture shows Stealth pilot Captain John W. Hesterman (Bandit #339) describing the cockpit functions of the F-117 to National Security Advisor Brent Scowcroft. (John Hesterman)

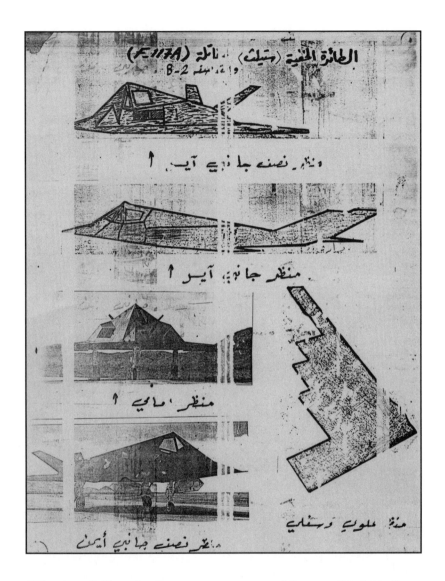

This aircraft identification page was removed from an Iraqi Air Force squadron Operations Building at Tallil Air Field by Major Luke Atwell. It had been duplicated on a crude copying machine and evidently passed out to all of the interceptor bases in Iraq. The two photographs at the bottom were taken from western magazines. More than likely, these pages were passed out to the Triple-A gunners as well. The silhouettes of the F-117 were to help the MiG pilots recognize them in the air. Although there were several close encounters between the MiG-23s and F-117s, the latter was never spotted by the Iraqis. (Luke Atwell)

previous strikes and all the Triple-A bursts. I knew I was in the right place, however, and released the weapon. As the target came into view, it quickly became apparent that someone had destroyed my target already! Not wanting to waste the bomb, I moved the target cursor over to hopefully crater a taxiway. On the way there, I got a little lucky and noticed a MiG-25 parked outside the hardened shelter. I put the cursor just behind the canopy, hoping I wasn't about to hit a cardboard decoy. A few seconds later I watched my 2000-pound GBU rip through the spine of the MiG, creating an impressive secondary explosion. After I returned to base and viewed my tape, the precision hit on the Iraqi fighter was confirmed and I was pleased with the outcome of the mission!"

The ability to alter a bomb's course, once it had exited the aircraft, made it a much more efficient weapon as related in the previous paragraphs. Within days of Hesterman's experience, a similar situation cropped up for Major Rich Treadway. He states, "We were going against quite a few of the airfields for several days. This particular (mission) was flown on 8 February against the hardened shelters at Tallil which is located in southern Iraq. Most of the big airfields were well protected by Triple-A and this one was one of the toughest to attack. Going against this one, piecemeal, only seemed to prolong the pain, so we were given the chance to take it out once and for all. A combined attack involving several non-stealth, night-precision bombers preceded us during the early hours of the night. After they finished, we launched twelve F-117s against the few dozen remaining shelters.

"I was the first aircraft in the strike package and I could clearly see the devastation wrought by the earlier attacks. On my first pass, I put a GBU-27 into the eastern half of a double structure (HAS). During the run, I noticed the shape of what appeared to be a Soviet-built 'Hind' helicopter parked outside the remaining half of the shelter. It was about this time that we all realized that the Iraqis were removing some of their aircraft from the shelters in the belief that parking them on an open ramp was safer than having them inside a targeted shelter. On my next pass, I aimed my bomb at the end of the shelter that was closest to the 'Hind.' When the bomb exploded, the over pressure blew out the multi-ton door and also destroyed the helicopter. It was very interesting to find out that a postwar inspection of that shelter by a bomb damage assessment team revealed the remains of a MiG-25 'Foxbat' inside. This made it a very satisfying mission to me; two bombs, two aircraft, and two shelters!"

While the Iraqi Air Force was being rendered ineffective and practically non-existent, the biggest threat that the Stealth would face was still at full strength and would remain so until the war ended. This threat was the Triple-A and SAMs located in and around Baghdad. No conventional aircraft were tasked with going in and knocking them out as they would have been toasted on the first attempt. The airspace over this "twilight zone" belonged to only two creatures of the night and they were the F-117 Nighthawk and the Tomahawk Cruise missile. During the day, it was relatively quiet within the city. Coalition Intelligence had put a figure of between 3500 and 4000 deadly gun barrels pointing skyward over this fortress. It was also determined that Baghdad contained over 60 SAMs. According to Major K.D. Boyer, the senior Electronic Weapons officer (EWO) in the Mission Planning Cell, "The Triple-A batteries totaled more than those that would have ringed Moscow during the height of the Cold War and the number of SAMs would have equaled what was on the Eastern Front (Warsaw Pact) from north of East Germany down to Czechoslovakia."

With the above figures in mind, you can try to visualize what the Stealth pilots saw and why they vividly recall what visually lay in front of them as they began lining up their targets over the city. The description given by Major "T-Pup" Treadway would be hard to top by any stretch of the imagination. "Ingress into the heavily defended target areas was always a spectacle. Although most of the airfields in southern Iraq seemed to be just as bad as Baghdad. CNN wasn't there, so it would be hard for everyone else to imagine, therefore I'll describe the obvious. As we approached Baghdad most nights, Triple-A from other, ongoing attacks would

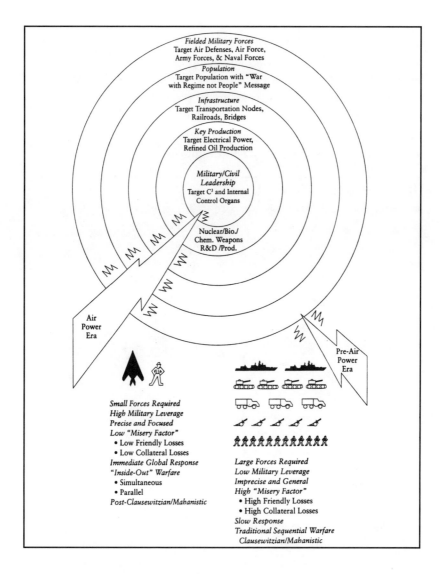

This diagram shows how the battle plan for Desert Storm worked. The Stealth aircraft and TLAMs started working from the center out. The priorities were higher as you got closer to the center of the circle. The Republican Guard and ground troop assets were the last targets to be taken out by airpower. The emphasis on the last phase was demonstrated right before the ground war began. By this time, the Iraqi control centers had been completely destroyed and the troops on the front lines had not been in touch with their leaders in Baghdad since the first two nights of the war. (Rod Shrader)

provide the eerie light show we were getting used to. It is hard to describe the sight; depending on sky conditions, you could see the orange glow for miles and miles. Closer into the city, the glow sharpened into the different colors of the competing types of ordnance being shot skyward. The 23mm looked like lines of bright orange fire. They spit upwards sometimes in snaky circles like someone wiggling the spray from a garden hose.

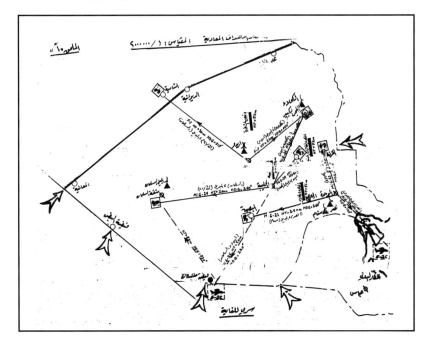

This diagram may be one of the most significant items that was retrieved from an Iraqi fighter squadron's operations building immediately after the war. What this appears to be is a detailed schematic of a plan to draw the Coalition air forces into a situation that would lure them across the border into Iraq. You can see that the Iraqi CAPs include the MiG-23s / -25s / and -29s. They would head straight for the border, in significant numbers, and at the last minute turn back. This would appear to be an attack into Saudi Arabia. Notice the position of the friendly AWACs aircraft along the Saudi border. This clearly shows that the MiG-25s would lead the thrust up to the border. The original diagram was retrieved by Major Luke Atwell while working with the 82nd Airborne Division in late February 1991. (Luke Atwell)

Although, the F-117 did not carry a wide range of ordnance, its capability of taking out just about any target in Iraq was attributed to the GBU-27, shown here. This was the ultimate deep penetrator for the Stealth. Note the sophisticated guidance system that has been attached to the nose of the bomb. This aircraft (#814) was named Final Verdict *and as this picture was taken, it was in the process of having its door art completed. By war's end, it had flown 34 combat missions.* (Ken Huff)

"The 57mm, fired by Soviet-made S-60s and ZSU-57s, seemed to float past and always reminded me of pink basketballs gliding by. The S-60s were shooting them in pairs and they looked like you could reach out and grab them. Depending on the fusing altitudes, they all seemed to explode like red and orange fireworks. The end result appeared like an incandescent bubble over the city ... strangely beautiful and incredibly dangerous!! I was always stunned by two facts. What we were seeing were just the tracers ... every seventh round, which meant that the sky was being saturated with seven times the metal we were witnessing. The other was that everything, and I mean everything, that was being shot up at us was then falling back down on to the city with the same or greater destructive force. This, no doubt, was resulting in all the collateral damage that the media kept attributing to us. The 57mm had an effective range of about 20,000 feet."

The Stealth pilots flew a wide variety of missions, but the emphasis was always on the targets that involved going "downtown." Before the war started, Iraq had hundreds of key assets that were well known to outside military planners. One can only imagine those assets that were never noticed or that Intelligence had to dig deep for. The long war with Iran had only served to deplete a small percentage of Iraq's manpower. Their stockpile of arms and ammunition wasn't really affected, at least not to the naked eye. One fact is for sure; Iraq was one solid, enormous

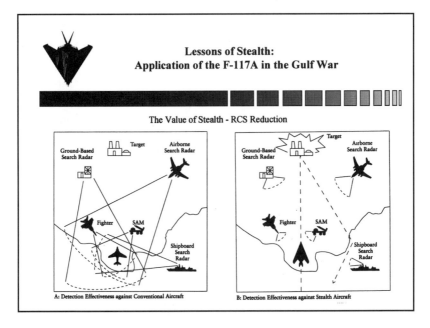

Both of these diagrams show just how valuable the F-117 was in penetrating Iraq's heavy air defense networks. Even with complete air superiority between the border and the target, conventional aircraft would have paid a high price in their efforts to destroy some of Iraq's key assets. The radar controlled SAMs and Triple-A would have provided a wall of deadly accurate fire which would have cost the Coalition forces many valuable lives and aircraft. The Stealth not only penetrated these, but destroyed the targets without getting so much as a scratch. (Rod Shrader)

armed camp from border to border. The wide variety of fighter bomber types that flew in all services of the Coalition hit just about every target within Iraq, with the exception of certain targets within the perimeter of Baghdad. With this in mind, it might be safe to say that the F-117s flew strikes against a larger number of key Iraqi assets than any other aircraft type. If you ever have the opportunity to talk at length with any of the Stealth pilots, you will find that when they relate to their most memorable missions, the airfields sorties always crop up. This is due to the fact that they were going against hostile aircraft types (mostly on the ground). Also, most of the major airfields were heavily defended with Triple-A and once the first bomb hit, the sky instantly lit up with deadly fireworks, just like over Baghdad. It is hard to comprehend how one would react when flying through total darkness and one second later you are swimming through a firestorm of deadly Triple-A. There is no way to know what you would do unless you had actually faced it.

Captain Mike "Slime" Mahan relates how he handled the rough ones. "Probably, the most memorable mission I flew was on 25 January. I was part of a large strike package that was tasked against several hardened-aircraft shelters at H-2 and H-3 airfields over in western Iraq. My first bomb run was over H-3 and at the same time some of us were hitting H-3, there was another group hitting H-2. As soon as each of us dropped the first ones, we headed for the opposite airfields with altitude deconfliction as we passed each other in the night. The weather was bad enough around these targets to force us to drop to a lower altitude in order to lock on. The thing that made it most memorable was the fact that the Triple-A fire was the most concentrated of any I can remember and that would include most of the missions I flew over Baghdad.

"Anyway, I headed into this solid wall of tracers and I'm thinking, o.k. there's all the stuff over on the left and then there's more over on the right, so there was no way to turn around and get the heck out of there, so I just concentrated on my target. It made me furious because there were so many guns firing at me!

It was this state of mind that helped get me through it. Another thing that I remember was how uncanny our accuracy and effectiveness was! Usually, if a target wasn't hit it was the result of a 'no-drop,' due to weather conditions. Generally, if a target was acquired and the bomb was dropped, there were very few cases where the bomb didn't hit exactly where it was supposed to. There were a few incidents, however, where the bomb didn't guide properly and this was due to a malfunction in the guidance system and not the fault of the pilot."

Most of the comments from the pilots involved the newer, tougher shelters. However, one of the pilots related his experience of demolishing one of the "antiquated" hangars that was located at a base near Baghdad. It was during a brief period two weeks into the war that the Stealth were being tasked to work over every known airfield in Iraq. The pilot's load on this mission consisted of two GBU-10s that would be dropped on an old 1950s type hangar that had rows of windows up at the top of each side. It also had a thin roof and was not built to withstand any type of explosives. At the time, it was jammed with many types of aircraft and the bombs hit on the near corner of the structure. The bombs detonated about the time they reached the floor of the hangar, disintegrating everything within. The fireball blew out the near set of doors and windows with the roof melting down in seconds. All of this happened while the pilot was still viewing it through his infrared. These types of older hangars were photographed after the war as just being a pile of ashes on a concrete surface.

One of the most memorable briefings given by General Schwarzkopf, on television, involved the famous "luckiest truck driver in Iraq." It showed the video of a truck crossing a bridge and just as it had cleared, a bomb hit dead center two seconds after the truck passed. This was from a video taken from one of the F-117s. Captain Jim Mastny was involved in one that was similar but maybe not so dramatic. Nevertheless, it had to be a "heart stopper" for the truck driver in question. "I know that several of our pilots made comments that they felt the Triple-A around some of the airfields was tracking them as they were shooting along behind them as they came over. I really don't think they tracked us on their radar, but they were probably tracking our sound which was the reason they were always behind us. Anyway, I certainly recall the 'lucky truck driver' video. Well, I can tell you that for every lucky one there were ten unlucky ones! My experience with a certain truck happened as I was attacking a hardened shelter at one of the airfields.

The seasoned ordnance personnel with the 37th worked some of the longest hours of any unit in Desert Storm. They had the responsibility of selecting the bombs that had been designated for that night's missions, bringing them into the shelter area, and matching up the right bombs with the right aircraft. There was also a certain amount of assembly that had to be completed on each bomb. There was a vast difference in the types of targets that would call for the GBU-27s as opposed to those requiring the GBU-10s. Their work began early in the day, when the coming night's orders had been received in the mission planning cell. It was then that the type of ordnance was selected for each target. (Rose Reynolds)

"My target was a specific shelter that was positioned by a sharp 90-degree curve in a service road. It was a concrete structure with a half-dome. Under it was an Iraqi aircraft. Our GBU-27s were designed to punch right through these and on into the floor. I'm striking from east to west, parallel to the runway and just as I release my bomb, I notice a small truck driving into the field of view of my infrared sensor and I'm watching my bomb and the time of fall before impact. I'm saying to myself that this guy is going to be in the middle of the bomb's explosion! He must have been doing slightly more than the speed limit for that road as he was turning the 90-degree curve. Just as the truck finishes making the curve, the bomb hits the shelter, blowing the doors out. The truck driver must have put the gas pedal to the floor, because he just barely missed the blast! I was relieved that he had made it and we are talking fractions of a second here. If he had been dozing slightly before the blast, he was wide awake now as he barreled out of my view at full speed. He was one of the lucky ones!"

Any story on Desert Storm would be incomplete if you didn't mention the electronic jammers: the EF-111A Ravens and the EA-6B Prowlers. These aircraft were borne out of lessons learned in the Vietnam War. They could lead a conventional strike force of aircraft into a heavily defended area, jam the defenses, allowing such non-stealthy aircraft as the F-16 and F/A-18 to reach the target, drop their ordnance, and get out safely. In other words, the electronic warfare (EW) aircraft are true force multipliers. They insure that those aircraft will live to fight again and again by emitting strong electronic signals that interfere with enemy radar and radio transmissions. But their association with the F-117 would be totally different. It is common knowledge that the Stealth fighter is not invisible, it just has very low radar visibility. In other words, they would not be dependent on an EW type to get them safely to the target, but that doesn't mean that the mission planners at Khamis didn't utilize the EF-111 to the maximum. They used it as the ultimate tool of deception and it worked perfectly, to their advantage.

The way this worked was to have the Ravens set up an orbit close to Baghdad. At a set time, they would begin jamming and this would trigger off a massive barrage of Triple-A. The Iraqis figured that when the jamming began, that the F-117s were in the vicinity and would be initiating their bomb runs. They were right on one assumption because the "Black Jets" were orbiting the area or inbound from the tankers. After several minutes of

Major Jerry Sink (Bandit #294) makes some last-minute checks before closing the canopy and taxing out for takeoff. With various pilots at the controls, this Stealth had already flown 22 missions over Iraq and Kuwait, indicating the war was probably close to three weeks old when this photo was taken. The 37th Wing was generating three waves of aircraft every night, which meant that some of them were flying twice in one night. This incredible rate was credited to the maintenance people and the Lockheed field representatives, who were in place to help with any problem that cropped up. (Rose Reynolds)

Major Joe Bouley gives a thumbs up to the ground crews as he taxies out for an early night mission. His aircraft, at this time, was working on its 22nd sortie over Iraq. Bouley was a key player in the Stealth Mission Planning Cell during the war and was also one of the eighteen 415th pilots who flew the first wave of aircraft over to the middle East. He was relatively new to the program with only about 50 hours in the aircraft when he flew over to Khamis Mushait in August 1990. (Rose Reynolds)

intense ground fire and no bomb explosions, things quieted down. By this time, the EF-111s had also exited their orbiting area. It was at this time that the F-117s made their moves. The attacks would be simultaneous, which meant that the bombs would impact on a wide variety of targets within seconds of each other, allowing the aircraft to exit the area before the Triple-A started back up.

Major Leatherman briefly explains the plans for the jammers beginning with Day One of the war. "As far as use of the EF-111 goes, I remember discussing this up at Riyadh one time during a planning session for that first night of the war. We asked to have some EFs jam for us as a deceptive tactic. It was a pretty big battle to get them to do this for two reasons. The CENTAF planners thought it would give our presence away to the Iraqis and the conventional aircraft needed them for survival. I told them that if they started jamming a few minutes prior to our time over target (TOT), they wouldn't be giving anything away. With a radar cross section like ours, we would be practically invisible, especially with all the blind Triple-A and SAM firing that was going on. We could almost guarantee that nobody could track a missile out to us. Our use of the EFs didn't last long due to the fact that the Iraqi IRADS had been reduced to rubble and there was very little need for jamming. Their gunners were not going to get any advance warning from their own radars, so why give them any from our side!"

Colonel Al Whitley, on the left, meets with some of the most influential people in the military and American government. To the left: Congressman Sam Nunn, Lt. General Charles A. Horner, Congressman John Warner, and unidentified. At this stage of the Gulf War, the interest in the F-117 was at an all-time high. These individuals were all privy to exactly how successful the aircraft had become, but the general public would not be completely enlightened until after the war had ended. This was taken at King Khalid Air Base, better known as Khamis Mushait, in Saudi Arabia. (Rose Reynolds)

Further details about using the EF-111 to complement Stealth operations will be discussed in the next chapter. At this point though, it would be appropriate to quote one of the senior EWO's who was flying right seat in one of the Ravens that was over Iraq

This is a picture of the original pass that was worn by Captain James Mastny, an F-117 pilot serving in Desert Storm. Every member of the 37th Fighter Wing organization, at Khamis, was required to wear these at all times. Each pass had the individual's photo on it. (James Mastny)

that first night. Lt. Fred Drummond, a senior Navy EWO on exchange with the 390th Electronic Combat Squadron, relates what he witnessed during the early hours of Desert Storm. His statement proves the value of stealth, especially when the skies are full of Iraqi MiGs capable of night intercepts with or without ground control (GCI). Keep in mind that the EF-111 and the F-117 carry no guns to defend themselves, thus they depend on either a low radar profile or a very low altitude to escape prying enemy radar. Drummond recalls, "Originally, four Ravens were going to provide jamming support for the first F-117 strike against targets in Baghdad. Due to the demand on our eighteen aircraft by the conventional strikers, the number dropped down to three. We took off from Taif, flew up to the tanker track and topped off. One by one, we headed south as we usually did. This time we took spacing and dropped down below Iraqi radar and reversed our

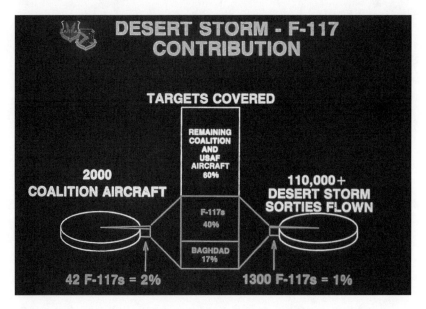

This diagram demonstrates the impact that only 42 F-117s had on the overall picture during Desert Storm. Note that of the 110,000 sortie total flown in the war by all Coalition aircraft, the Stealth only flew one percent. However, they took out the majority of the high-value Iraqi assets in Baghdad, which was the most heavily-defended city in the world. (Rob Donaldson)

The scene was shot at Tallil Airfield right after the cease-fire. A demolition charge was detonated in the cockpit of this MiG-23 to make sure nothing could be salvaged from it. It had been damaged by a previous night attack on the airfield complex. During the first two nights of the war, there were a number of MiG-23s flying CAPs over the city of Baghdad. Their numbers dwindled quickly, once the F-15 Eagles began prowling the skies over Iraq. (Luke Atwell)

course to the north. As we egressed into Iraq, we could see the explosions of the forward radar complexes being taken out. Right after this was when the trouble began. Just as we turned on 070 degree heading towards Baghdad, one of the AWACS broadcast a bogey call. It was heading directly for us. It was a MiG-29 and it over flew us as we were hugging the ground.

"Our AWACS continued to call out hostile MiGs in the area. There were a lot of them flying the barrier patrols between the Saudi border and Baghdad. Another of our Ravens was being stalked by a MiG-25. At this time, our number three aircraft decided to pop up and began jamming a little early in an effort to draw all the MiGs over his way, thus allowing the remaining two to get in and set up. All three of us were flying separate, unconnected tracks and maintaining radio silence. It was a great plan, but unfortunately, not all of the enemy fighters followed along. They kept us busy, but by staying low to the ground, we were able to stay away from them. Later in the night, the F-15 Eagles began their successful efforts to clear the skies of Iraqi aircraft, but since we were up before that, we caught the brunt of what they had to offer. This also reinforced the value of stealth, because if the 3 A.M. strikers had been conventional, they would have been in trouble before they reached Baghdad! I can vividly recall in the nights that followed, when we were on station jamming for the F-15E Strike Eagles, I looked out in the distance to see the city lit up with a solid blanket of Triple-A and the periodic explosions in the midst of it. It was the F-117s hitting their targets in an area where no other aircraft would have survived."

As mentioned earlier, a handful of 417th instructor pilots came over right after the war started and they quickly worked themselves into the mission rotation. Every Stealth pilot who flew combat in the Gulf War had to go through all the electrified tension which was better known as the "first mission." Jim Mastny (Bandit #268) tells about his first mission and at the time, it was not the least bit humorous. "The first mission for me was almost two weeks into the war. We had come over after it started so we were due a few sorties within Saudi airspace to familiarize ourselves with the terrain and all the procedures that went with the job. It took about a week to get through the spin-up. I think it ended up being from 5-7 days before we got into combat after we had arrived at Khamis. I asked as many of the 415th and 416th guys about their first missions and they all said the same thing ... nerve wracking!

"On my first mission, I was coming off the tanker and in the distance I see the Kuwaiti oil fields on fire. I am flying northbound and all of a sudden the aircraft turns to an eastbound heading. (The aircraft's route was preprogrammed and the computer was flying that course.) Now, I look ahead and see all the fires. They are out in the distance and look like a small yellow ball and they had been out the right front side of the cockpit! My mind looks out and tells me those might be SAMs launched against me. Then after a few moments, I realize that the ball of fire is not going away and that is a bad sign! All of this took place in a time frame of 30 seconds. Then, I realized what I had been told that if it doesn't move in your windscreen, it's following you!! Here I am on my first mission and I'm getting a SAM shot at me. Suddenly, my aircraft turns to the north (as it had been programmed to do). This made the light disappear and then I knew it was from the fires in the oil field and not a SAM. It was a great relief to me, but what I had just witnessed was realistic and it certainly dominated my attention for a brief period."

A few of the Stealth pilots witnessed impressive secondary explosions as did the F-111F aircrews. Most were generated by well-placed bombs on jammed ammunition bunkers. However, on a few occasions these were generated by the Iraqis themselves, brought about by either incompetence or a run of bad luck. Most of the big secondaries were briefly mistaken for nuclear explosions, especially by the Stealth pilots who were off in the distance. Major Wes Wyrick recalls one that he witnessed while returning from a mission against a television station on the west side of Iraq. "On the way back from a long mission over on the west side, I passed close to two major airfields at H-2 and H-3. This was early on in the war and there were still a few MiGs capable of flying, so I kept a sharp eye out as I passed over. After being on oxygen for so long, my night vision was excellent. I also knew that there had been some Scuds launched against Israel from this area. As I passed over, there was a low cloud cover over both airfields. An instant later there was a bright flash of light that was exaggerated due to the clouds. It was some type of explosion and it was definitely big! In the back of my mind, I figured it was a nuclear explosion that had been carried out by Israel in retaliation for the Scud attacks.

"With my radio out, I had no way of learning any accurate information on what I had just seen. As I crossed the border, I put out the antennae and called the AWACS by secure radio. I told them what I had seen and they interrupted by saying, 'We know' and that's all I could get out of them. After landing back at Khamis, I went to debrief and that's when I picked up the real story. It seems that the Iraqis had launched another Scud and it had malfunctioned soon after launch, blowing up at about 2000 feet altitude. What an explosion! The flight back from the H-2 area to home base was a long one! I can recall one other mission that involved a large explosion and I created it with a well-placed GBU-10 . It was against a two-story building that was involved in producing arms. I dropped my bomb right into the middle of the

Some of the critical jobs within the Stealth Wing were highly specialized. The ordnance people were as well trained as any in the USAF. They handled a large number of GBU-10s and GBU-27s during the brief 43 day war. It wasn't the destructive power of the 2,000-pound bomb that made it such a lethal weapon when delivered by the F-117. It was its Texas Instruments guidance kit inside the seeker head on the nose of the bomb that gave these weapons their precision capabilities. In this picture, the ordnance specialists are carrying the guidance units for the bombs which were shipped into Saudi Arabia in these protective containers. From there, they were mated with the bombs and loaded on the aircraft for delivery against key targets within Iraq. (Rose Reynolds)

building and it blew up immediately. One of our F-117s was trailing ten minutes behind me. By the time he passed over the target, he later reported the column of smoke had reached approximately 25,000 feet."

Covering a wide path all over Iraq, there were very few, if any, targets that could escape the marauding F-117s. Once the air defenses and communication centers had been blinded, the Stealth concentrated on a wide variety of enemy assets. After

The Iraqi Air Force owned a wide variety of Soviet-built aircraft when the Gulf War started. Most of these had survived the war with Iran. Their arsenal included the MiG-21, MiG-23, MiG-25, and the MiG-29. Shown here is a MiG-21 that was parked away from the shelters at Tallil, when it received minor damage. It sat in this position for the remainder of the short war, but when the demolition crews from the 82nd Airborne noticed it, the fighter was destroyed with explosives. Notice the Soviet Atoll air-to-air missile that is still attached to the left pylon. (Luke Atwell)

talking with numerous pilots about their missions, it appears that all of them tried their hand at "bridge busting." Most of these targets were not as well defended as the ones in Baghdad, but nevertheless, it was very challenging to render them useless by dropping them into the water. One of the most spectacular hits was recorded by Major Joseph Salata while flying a mission in his aircraft #839 named *Grim Reaper*. He recalls the details, "I remember the night of 9 February 1991 very well. My target was what we called the 'July 14th Memorial Bridge' in Baghdad (another of the many memorials of Saddam's take over). Jerry Leatherman was hitting the same target several minutes before me. As we studied the photo, we noticed that it was a suspension bridge. We decided that in order to do the most serious damage, we'd have to place a bomb right on top of one of the supports. We also knew that the winds were going to be heavy, in fact, probably a big-time left cross wind due to the run-in heading we were using. Jerry said he'd aim for the top center of the near support and I would have to judge my aiming off of his bomb's impact.

"As I approached the bridge, I noticed that his bomb had missed a little to the right due to the high winds. In fact, it almost looked like someone had just taken a bite out of the right side of the structure. To correct for the winds, I aimed way over to the left and my bomb impacted the far right side of the support. For an instant, nothing happened and I thought that I hadn't caused much damage. Suddenly, the entire bridge started moving downwards! The entire thing fell into the river, causing a huge splash on either side, from shore to shore. I let out a loud yell in the cockpit and I remember thinking that I couldn't wait to get back to base and let the rest of the guys view my tape!"

For the majority of the Gulf War, the selection of targets would originate at the top and come down through channels to the Stealth mission planners. In turn, the type of ordnance needed to kill the prescribed targets were always selected by the weapons specialists within the F-117 Wing. There were a few, but short-lived variations in this set-up. Major Shrader explains, "We usually selected the bombs/weapon types that we were going to drop on a target. The frag (target orders) would come down and we would handle it from there. Apparently somebody at CENTAF decided that this was not acceptable and that they would start assigning the weapons to be used on the targets coming down in the daily frag. I was amazed when I first saw this come down! They had selected a GBU-27 for a bridge! Well, by now you know that this specific bomb is a deep penetrator. What happens when you hit a bridge with this weapon is that it would put a small hole in the bridge, go straight through and explode before it hit the water. Nothing would happen to the bridge. I immediately called CENTAF up and explained to them what would happen, but they decided that I should follow the orders as they had come down.

"I covered this with Colonel Whitley and he understood my point, but orders were orders. So, we went against the bridges with the GBU-27s. The bombs hit dead center on the bridge, went right on through, and the Iraqi trucks drove around the hole. I collected the strike film for the night and sent it up to CENTAF. I picked out one in particular and added a note that said, 'What you see here is a GBU-27's effect on a bridge. Notice the small hole that it made.' The next night the frag came down and with it was a note that said, 'Use weapons as desired.' We won a minor point for the weapons officers in the Wing and in turn, we were able to be more effective against the remainder of the bridges that were being concentrated on during the final stages of the war."

The 417th Squadron pilots who came over after the war started were too late to join in on the initial attacks against the heavily defended targets in Baghdad, but there were plenty of assets left to bomb when they did work into the mission rotation. Although they could see that all of the aircraft had come through without a scratch, there was still that doubt in their minds until they had the first mission under their belt. Captain Kenneth Huff (Bandit #275) recalls every detail of his first mission after arriving from Tonopah. His targets for that first night were two major bridges. "My first experience flying the F-117 in combat was on the night of 1 February. It is still very clear in my memory. After the standard briefing, I remember my 417th squadron commander, Lt. Colonel Bob Maher, impressing upon me that I did not have to deliver my bombs that night if the target weather was questionable. He told me how it was his third sortie in Vietnam before he finally got to drop his bombs and not to press my luck! Maybe he knew more about me than I did. I remember being really nervous about that mission until I got my engines started and then it was just like any other sortie.

"My targets that night were two bridges, one on the Tigris River and one on the Euphrates River at Samawah and An Nasiriyah. I would be dropping GBU-10s on each of them. Going into the first target area I was watching what was going on off to my right side. I was fascinated watching the Triple-A flying up from down the river and mentally making notes as to the caliber it was. Nothing was coming up around my aircraft, so I thought this was going to be a cakewalk! I got set up on my target run, all systems were working fine, and my timing was perfect. I threw my cursor out to the target and sure enough, it was on a bridge. This was sure a lot easier than the training mission targets we used to task ourselves with! I was aiming at the center of three bridges in the IRADS sensor display, but my photo pack for my first target showed only one bridge. Now what?? In the confusion, I took a little longer than I should have, but I remembered the second target photo pack and sure enough there were three bridges there. Intel had mixed up the order of my photos. I managed to figure this out quickly and drop the bridge. Then all hell broke loose!! The Triple-A was everywhere. Fortunately, it was what we referred to as "bomb-activated," so I was nearly out of range before it started coming up. The second bridge that night was easy since I had the correct photos to compare my display with. Just like the first target, things were uneventful until the bomb impacted. This had been my first sortie into Iraq and it was my most memorable."

Day 6 and Day 7 of the war were some of the most intense and successful ones for the Stealth Wing. A large portion of the strike force was sent against select targets in Baghdad, but a number of F-117s went up against the heavily defended Balad Southeast Airfield. This complex was known to house a large number of MiGs and it was also ringed with deadly Triple-A. It was considered a "high-risk" target to any aircraft that attacked. Major Joe Bouley remembers a mission where Coalition Intel had determined that a number of Iraqi aircraft had been loaded with chemical weapons. (This scenario repeated itself several times during the war). "This particular mission was on a Thursday, 22 January 1991. My call sign for the mission was Ice-Zero-5. We were set up to hit the big airfield near Baghdad called Balad Southeast and the mission would last over six hours. It was a heavily defended, multi-reveted fighter base. It seems that our Intel guys up at Riyadh had picked up some info that a lot of Iraqi aircraft — Fencers, MiGs, etc. — had been loaded with chemicals, so we were fragged (ordered to hit a specific target) to get in there and take out as many of these hazards as we could. We used 2000 pounders with delayed fusing. Jerry Leatherman was to be my wingman. We took off at 6:39 P.M., joined up with the tanker and made the two-hour flight to the border.

"We topped off and dropped down, heading north into enemy air space at precisely the time we were supposed to. It was going to be a coordinated attack on the airfield. There would be others going in ahead of us. As we approached the area, up ahead, we could see bombs going off and a lot of Triple-A fire. To me, it looked like 57mm and a couple of SAMs. It was an impressive light show! I hit my IP as I was coming in looking at my infrared and trying to pick out my target. I could see other revetments on the airfield in close proximity to mine being hit. I swung around so I could come in on the target from the northeast for a bomb run to the southwest. There was all kinds of stuff going off underneath me. I found my target, dropped the bomb dead-on, and then we were supposed to do a re-attack. I lined up and came in, dropped the second bomb, and it was supposed to go out at ground-zero, but didn't. I quickly realized that I had a hung bomb and not only that, my bomb bay door was stuck open!! I was able to get it closed and then I egressed out of the area with my hung bomb.

Captain Rob Donaldson moves in under a KC-135 to refuel his F-117 while flying from Oshkosh '91 to McConnell AFB, Kansas for an air show. The Gulf War had only been over for a few months and the demand for the Stealth at the various Air Force Bases for their open houses was at an all-time high. Below the nose of the F-117 is an F-16 that was piloted by a friend of Donaldson, Lt. Guy Bower, who was flying out of McConnell with the Kansas ANG. (Rob Donaldson)

"Like I mentioned before, we always had a secondary target. Mine was a bridge in the general area as my primaries. I knew that my system was working o.k., so if the bomb would release, I knew I could guide it down for a good hit. I lined it up, the bomb bay doors opened, and the bomb released, scoring a bulls-eye on the bridge. Leatherman was following me as he was to be the last man off the targets and he had the secondary (bridge) on his infrared, when the bomb exploded. He got everything on his tape, so it was exciting to watch it on video when we got back. It was very rewarding to me to know that I had been able to effectively get rid of the hung bomb and hit the bridge."

This is an excellent picture that shows both of the F-117's GBU bombs loaded and ready for a mission. In a majority of the missions that were flown, these bombers only used one bomb at a time, enabling them to destroy two separate targets, which could be up to twenty minutes apart. At times, there were several of these aircraft flying over Baghdad at the same time. Each had assigned altitudes and speeds, which eliminated the chance of mid-air collisions over targets that were in close proximity. This was taken outside of a hardened shelter at Khamis Mushait. (Ken Huff)

With the exception of ground troops and armor, the F-117 was called upon to hit just about every type of target that was up for grabs during the final thirty days of the war. For a very brief period, they were even used to hunt Scuds, which was a total waste of the aircraft's potential. They had no luck in this endeavor. Of course, finding these mobile missile launchers was like looking for a needle in a haystack. But, the F-117 did excel in a dangerous assignment that it had no expertise in and that was playing the part of a "Wild Weasel." It seems that some of the

SAM sites were so heavily defended that the F-4G Wild Weasels couldn't even get close enough to take them out. To complicate things, these select sites were defending high-value assets that the conventional aircraft were tasked with taking out. Thus, the call went out for the F-117s.

Captain Rob Donaldson was in one of the strike packages of Stealth aircraft sent out to kill these SAM sites. He states, "The F-117 was supposed to be a tactical fighter aircraft, but we struck a large number of strategic targets in Iraq. For a while, we even took on the role of Wild Weasel. I specifically remember one night when ten F-117s went after an equal number of SAM sites. These were located on the west/northwest corner of Baghdad and were right in the way of the B-52s that were trying to get to the big armored facility nearby. I think it was one of the biggest military complexes in Iraq and that is why it was so well defended.

"We went ten for ten that night, taking out the SA-2 and SA-3 sites. The B-52s were coming right behind us and before the smoke had cleared, they dumped hundreds of bombs on the facility. They came through completely unscathed. We were also used in a reconnaissance role, flying over some of the targets that had been taken out previously by the day bombers. We turned our cameras on and over flew them. We were able to determine if the Iraqis had repaired anything. They were clever, however! On some of their hardened-aircraft shelters, they would go out and paint black 'holes' on the tops of some that had not been bombed. This made it appear, to standard aerial reconnaissance, that it had already been destroyed. This ploy did not work because there were people at HQ who were charged with very specifically counting and being accountable for each aircraft shelter that was hit. Each time we landed back at our base, we took the film out of our aircraft and reviewed it with the Intel people. At that time, that specific HAS was marked off as destroyed. The film was always loaded on to a Learjet and immediately flown up to Riyahd. We became very versatile in a wide variety of missions."

Captain Kenneth Huff (Bandit #275) is shown here in front of his F-117 at Khamis. Huff was an instructor pilot in the 417th Squadron and was in the cadre of pilots that brought the last group of aircraft over during the first few days of the war. He flew his first combat mission over Iraq on the first of February and ended up with twelve missions by the time the war ended. (Ken Huff)

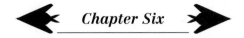

Chapter Six

Unleashing Multi-Ship Attacks

If you were to make a list of the outstanding accomplishments of the F-117 during the Gulf War, at the very top would be a tactic designed and perfected after the war had begun. It was something that had never been tried before and certainly never heard of in all the history of aerial warfare. This phenomenon became known, within Stealth circles, as the simultaneous, multi-ship attack. Had it not been for the advanced technology built into the F-117 and the skill of its pilots, it would never have been attempted. But, in the span of a few short weeks, it was not only attempted, but perfected and utilized as one of the most deadly strike tactics to emerge from Desert Storm. In simple terms, it was a multi-ship attack (as many as 16 F-117s) that converged on a single target, from all directions. They all dropped their bombs at the same time and all impacted within 1.5 seconds; and it was done in total darkness with no radio communication between the aircraft!

The strategy of the multi-ship strike was twofold. First of all, if there were any high-value targets (a series of targets clustered close together) that were heavily defended, the impact of 32 2000-pound bombs at the same time would most probably eliminate any complex they hit. Secondly, the aircraft would already be out of the immediate area when the bombs impacted. Any Triple-A activity after the bombs went off, would be useless against the striking aircraft. Of course, if one aircraft went in too early, the rest would be at a higher risk. Keep in mind that there was a very small separation in altitude between the aircraft so the chance of a mid-air collision was eliminated.

Mike Mahan reflects on this concept. "We did quite a lot of multi-ship attacks which contained up to 16 aircraft. We would have a very small altitude separation between the aircraft as they came across the target or target group. (When I say group, you are still talking about a pretty tight area). It was extremely important that everyone adhere to their briefed parameters; be on your altitude, be on the briefed altimeter setting, and be on time! This required superior discipline and there again, our training allowed us to do that. Working for a precise time of weapons delivery was something we always prided ourselves on. All of this was 'com out.' Also, if the weather was bad and you had to go down to another altitude, you had alternate altitude procedures for getting down to where you had to be and ways that the egress and ingress routes were deconflicted for all that. It ended up being very complex for the planners to plan. But, we tried to make it as simple as possible for the pilots who were flying it. On the timing, you didn't want to be the early one going in there because your buddies would let you know about it when you got back. If you were early, the Triple-A kicked up and the rest caught the brunt of it. Usually, our TOTs (time over target) were within a couple of seconds!"

There weren't many targets left in the Iraq/Kuwait theatre that would warrant such a massive strike. Every Stealth pilot who participated remembers it well. Toward the end of the war, there was a huge building in Baghdad that housed some key government offices. It covered a significant area such as a city block. The objective was to take it down with one strike that would consist of 18 F-117s hitting it at the same time. Jerry Leatherman was in on the multi-ship mission, "This complex covered a wide area and we planned on destroying it with separate waves of 18 aircraft at a time. We basically launched, in two waves, every airplane we had.

"The first night we were fighting some severe storms in and around Baghdad. In our minds, this mission was a waste of time because the war was going so well for the Coalition, but orders were orders. Our weather people forecasted some nasty stuff over the target and it turned out to be worse than we anticipated. We kept dropping down lower and lower trying to acquire the target, but to no avail. Well, only one of us actually dropped his bomb and only one at that. With the close proximity of the aircraft and the weather the way it was, it was a dangerous mission and a waste of time. But, there is a bright side. The next night the weather cleared and we put up 18 aircraft and totally destroyed the target. It was a pretty spectacular show!"

On Day 23 of the war (7-8 February), the usual three waves of F-117s hit a wide variety of targets with great success. Even with marginal weather conditions in some of the target areas, most of the assigned assets were destroyed. The second wave of the night was a significant point in the war, because the 37th Wing dropped the 1000th bomb of the war. The honor went to Scott "Outlaw" Stimpert of the 416th Squadron. He relates that night from his point of view, "Our target that night was the Samarra Chemical Works facility west of Baghdad. I had been assigned two targets within this complex. These were probably some of the toughest hardened shelters that we ran up against during the war. Not only were they state-of-the-art, but the Iraqis had bulldozed a large amount of dirt on top of them, so it was difficult to identify IR-wise and difficult to get into because it was well defended by Triple-A.

"I dropped the bombs, with very little reaction from their gunners. My log book describes it as light. The bombs impacted exactly where they were supposed to with no problem. I fly back to Khamis, taxi in, and as I nose into the parking spot, Colonel Whitley is standing in my Tab-V, feet spread, hands crossed over his chest, staring at my aircraft as I rolled in. Now, if you know the Colonel, he is not the guy you would want waiting on you. My mind was racing through possible ways I could have 'screwed up' so bad that word had gotten back to the base before I did!! Just as my aircraft comes to a stop, I notice there are others standing around and one of them has a sign that says, '1000th bomb dropped.' Turns out that I was the one who dropped the milestone bomb for the 37th. They were counting guys who came back, based on TOTs, who had weather and who didn't, who got to drop and who didn't. It turns out that one of my bombs was it."

If you can get a Stealth pilot to talk about some of the missions he flew, most of the ones that are still vivid in their memories deal with targets in Baghdad or the major airfields. But, there were some that they tackled that were so deep into Iraq that they could not carry enough fuel to make it back out. In order to pull this off, they could only do one thing ... take the tankers with them! These missions were living nightmares because they were usually still in Iraqi airspace when the sun came up and the length of time in the cockpit made it very uncomfortable. Nonetheless, these had to be carried out. The targets were remote (up close to the Turkish border), but heavily defended. Since the aircraft types operating out of Turkey had no Stealth capabilities, these missions were "dealt to the Stealth."

Flying these was tough, but it was even worse to try and plan them. Major K.D. Boyer gives some insight to the problems involved. "The very long-range missions that were flown up on the Turkish border brought up a lot of problems. One of those involved the use of tankers. If you bring a big aircraft like a KC-10 into hostile airspace and it is filled with fuel, it isn't very fast or maneuverable (empty or full). These guys were hanging it out, to say the least when they had to fly deep into Iraq. It is quite an undertaking to bring multiple tankers in just west of Baghdad in order to do a final refueling of the F-117s before they made the long flight north, up in the Mosul area.

"Without complete control of the skies, it would have been impossible because they have such a distinct radar profile. Now, when the fighters were topping off, it would not take a rocket scientist to figure out that they were there for a purpose and since nothing else was showing up on radar, you would have to figure that there were F-117s close by. Once the tankers finished pumping the gas, they got on the fast track back to the Saudi border! After the final refueling, the F-117s head straight for their distant targets. With limited fuel onboard, there is none

This picture only shows a small portion of the F-117s that will form up the first wave of the night. In order to put three waves up in one night, the first had to launch before dark for the 2.5 hour flight to the Iraqi border. The third and final wave usually had a tight schedule in order to make it back across the border before first light. Everything that the Stealth did, was based on precise timing. (Rose Reynolds)

available for maneuvering or diverting off of the straight line. Also, they must locate the target fast as there is no fuel for multiple passes. If the winds aren't exactly as predicted, then the pilot has a potential problem. Fortunately, we were able to pull off several of these missions, but without the F-15s clearing the skies, it could have been disastrous."

Major Rod Shrader was one of the pilots who flew missions up to the Turkish border. He remembers a four-ship that he was part of. "One of those long missions involved four of us. Because of the length of the mission, we actually had to drag the tanker with us for quite some distance into Iraq. What was significant about the target area that Phil McDaniel and I had was that there was really no photo of it available. We had a terrain picture, then we had a drawing on that photo of a square and a trail leading up to that square! There was no doubt that this target Intel was from a human and not a U-2 camera. All of this was rather unusual because we were used to very good imagery as to exactly what we were striking, so we had no idea what this target would look like. We just knew where the point of impact was to be on the side of this mountain.

"As we met the tanker to go across the border, I was on the left wing tip (about four feet away) and all of a sudden it just went black. It caught me by surprise, because the tanker pilot turned off all his lights the moment he crossed over into Iraq. Being that I couldn't see a thing, I had to pull away from my last known position of the wing tip. By this time, my antennae had been retracted as we were all stealthed up. I had to extend them, so I could explain to the tanker pilot that I did not have X-ray vision and that he would have to turn his lights on. He turned them up just enough to let us top off our tanks and we launched on the mission.

"En route to the target area ... as we started our orchestrated strike there and I came in from the IP, I had no idea what we would find and how difficult it would be to see. Well, the cursor lined up on this huge building. I think it might have been a structure that was occupied by the Iraqi Air Force. It was so big that I couldn't miss it. Again, a beautiful INS. What was significant about all of this was that it was to be a re-attack, which is very dangerous, especially if the target has a lot of Triple-A around it. We had to plan this very carefully so McDaniel and I planned to do a simultaneous attack on the second pass, within a second of each other. It ended up that the bombs struck the target within a half second of each other so it went even better than we had planned. We picked up our tankers at the border with our fuel extremely low."

All during the 1980s, there was one target in Iraq monitored with great interest from both Israel and the United States: the Baghdad Nuclear Research Facility. This deadly complex could have been a major threat to any country within range of the

Scuds, so in the early 1980s, Israel successfully bombed it to make sure it was put out of business. Needless to say, with the cash flow coming into Iraq from oil revenues, it was put back in working order. It also had to be in the top five assets for the Iraqi government so it was ringed with SAMs and numerous other Triple-A weapons.

One of the 415th Squadron pilots recalls the efforts made by the Stealth organization, to neutralize it. Major Joe Bouley states, "It was kind of interesting to watch the target list changes as the progress of the war went on. I remember a large attack force was supposed to hit the nuclear complex. I believe it was two squadrons of F-16s that were going to hit it. They came in low and tried to do 'pop-up' maneuvers on it. They were forced to release their bombs too early because of the intense ground fire and SAM launches and a couple of their aircraft were shot down. The bombs that did reach the complex fell on the large dirt berms that had been bulldozed up around the facility. No damage was done and the cost of the attack had been high. That very night, we got orders to hit the complex immediately. The cell worked up a plan and hit every building in the facility, including the reactors. They never knew we were coming until the bombs exploded. This, once again, proved that with the Stealth getting in undetected and taking out a well-defended target, the lives of a lot of pilots and valuable equipment was saved."

Only a small, select group of pilots will ever know the feelings and emotions that were awakened while flying through a hail of Triple-A fire in total darkness over one of the most heavily defended areas in the world. Many do not care to talk about it and that is understandable. One thing for sure, they all developed an instant appreciation for things that we all take for granted. Perhaps, Major Lorin Long (Bandit #290) can sum it up best as he briefly recalls a few things about his first mission which was flown on Night One and his comments on what he thought about on his return. "I was assigned to lead a two-ship to a target just south of Baghdad which consisted of suspected chemical weapons storage bunkers. The strike was at 0500.

Major Mike Mahar was my wingman that night. I flew aircraft #842 which went by the name of *Hammer Time*. It was actually assigned to Captain Rich Cline, but I was flying it this night. Right off, I had an INS problem in the arming area, but was able to correct it and proceed.

"The route to the target area was uneventful, but I could see Baghdad from 60 miles or more. The Triple-A that the first wave had stirred up was unbelievable. However, it was moderate in the area we were hitting. I tried to disregard the air bursts and was able to successfully concentrate on an accurate weapons release and target tracking. We hit our objective and the flight back to the tankers went off as planned. I do remember that there was a lot of fog around Khamis when I arrived back in the area about 0800. I also remember that the sunrise was beautiful and it was something that I had wondered if I would ever see again. I really felt like my life had changed after my first exposure to combat and getting shot at. Colonel Whitley had told us to expect this feeling. I'll tell you something else that had a profound effect on me that morning. As I taxied back to my parking slot after the mission, all the ground crews and support people were lined up on the taxiways and they all saluted as I went past. This was a very emotional time for me."

The Gulf War ended after only 43 days. Hundreds of thousands of military personnel contributed their best efforts to see it to a successful conclusion. But, when the dust settled, it was the F-117 that stood out above all the others. Lest any of us forget, the Stealth force only represented 2.5% of the total Coalition air assets, in theatre. However, in the first 24 hours of the war, they struck 31% of all the targets that were hit during that period.

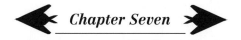

Chapter Seven

Mission Planning

From the early days of World War II, the job of mission planning has been critical to the success of any squadron or group. It is an area that has no glamour and very little excitement, and the pressure is excessive due to the fact you have a lot of lives depending on the best possible strike packages. By the time Desert Shield / Desert Storm rolled around in 1990, the basics remained the same, but sophistication of the threats had grown tenfold. You might say that the name of the game remained the same but all of the rules had changed. The accuracy of the Triple-A and the radar guided surface-to-air missiles had improved so much since Vietnam. If a mission planning unit did not have current Intelligence on threats that existed along the strike routes, they were all but out of business and the success of the mission was compromised.

The Mission Planning Cell (MPC) was, and still is, critical to the F-117's success against the more heavily guarded enemy assets. The routes that the Stealth had to fly to get into Baghdad were among the toughest that any aircraft type had ever attempted to penetrate. There are three essential components that make up the MPC: Intelligence Specialists, Electronic Warfare Officers (EWOs), and a select number of Stealth pilots. The Intelligence people (primarily) determined how many defensive systems were deployed, where they were located, what types of systems they were, provided very accurate target coordinates to the planning cell, and procured and maintained all the imagery and maps. Then, working closely with the weapons officers, Intel determined which of the two bomb types should be used against each target. They also had to know exactly which targets were at the top of the priority list and exactly why they were to be hit.

The EWOs had the responsibility of determining which was the best route to and from the target once the aircraft had crossed into hostile airspace. They based their planning on the data that Intel had given to them.

As mentioned many times before, the F-117 is known to the general public and the media as the invisible aircraft. This is not entirely true, but the Stealth does have a very minute radar signature which makes it difficult to track accurately. It would be very difficult to bring one down, but it could be done. So if the risk is at best minimal, then you can put in an aggressive, professional team of mission planners that have all the up-to-date Intel and you have just about eliminated the risk factor. This only leaves the chance of a random hit or the "Golden BB" (the bullet that has your name on it), which will always be there regardless of what type of weapons system you put out there in harm's way!

Within days after the 415th Squadron landed at Khamis Mushait, the mission planners had already worked out most of the details for the first two nights of the war. Of course the list of targets were always fluid and they changed every few days. This wasn't a case of being indecisive. The complicated list of Iraqi threats changed every day, and as Coalition Intelligence picked up these changes from their U2 flights and Satellite surveillance, then the adjustments were passed to the Stealth planners. The list of targets that were being selected came from CENTAF and only on a few occasions did a specific target originate at the squadron level. Even then, they had to be approved by upper management in Riyadh.

The pilots involved in mission planning were all weapons officers in the squadrons and/or wing. Two of the pilots with access to top secret intelligence coming out of Riyadh were Major Jerry Leatherman and Captain Marcel Kerdavid. Rounding out the planning cell was an experienced EWO, Major K.D. Boyer and the 415th Squadron's Major Joe Bouley and Captain Dennis Baker. This group was instrumental in firming up the strike plans for Night One of the upcoming Gulf War. There were countless prac-

After Desert Storm ended, the demand for the Stealth fighter on the Air Show / Open House circuit was phenomenal. This was taken at NAS Memphis in October 1991 the day before the Open House. This 416th Fighter Squadron F-117 was assigned to and flown by Desert Storm veteran, Major Rod Shrader. He is shown here after making a couple of high speed passes over the field, taxiing up to the designated area where the expected crowds could view this "super star" of the Gulf War. (Warren E. Thompson)

tice missions scheduled out of Khamis and these were basically planned by Major Bouley and his staff. The EWOs were more concerned with planning the strike routes inside Iraq which would be littered with sophisticated Triple-A (Anti-Aircraft Artillery) and SAMs (Surface-to-Air Missiles).

With the sophistication of threats possessed by Iraq, one of the most vital components of the planning cell was the EWO. The EWO understood every type of radar known to be used by Iraq and knew which ones might have the best chance of detecting the incoming F-117s. The EWO's job was to plan the routes so that these threats would be avoided. The plans were only as good as the Intelligence that was being passed down from

CENTAF. The Chief Mission Planner / EWO that was assigned to Stealth operations was Major K.D. Boyer who had learned his trade as a back seater in the F4G Wild Weasels. He recalls the very early days right after news of the invasion reached the Stealth community at Tonopah. "We really began planning just hours after we received word that Iraq had invaded Kuwait. By the time we arrived over in Saudi on a C-5 Galaxy, we had six major targets already planned out in detail. For all we knew, the war would start right after we got over there. Four of these targets were in and around Tallil and the reasoning behind this was due to the fact that this airfield was in close proximity to Saudi Arabia and it possessed a large number of fighter aircraft. It was also a major communications and intercept operations sector within the Iraq defense complex. It covered the entire southeastern portion of Iraq.

"Once we established our planning cell at Khamis, we continued to 'tweak' the plans for the first few nights. By late September, we had all of Night One planned for the entire Wing. Thirty days later we had Night Two nailed down. We were told not to plan out much further than the second or third night because there was a chance that we would have to go back in on some of the same targets to completely destroy them. The exact battle plan for the first two nights was fluid due to the constant Intelligence updates we were receiving. I might add here that our Intel people were some of the sharpest I had ever come in contact with. By the time that the Gulf War actually began, only about two targets, from the original list, survived all the changes. This was due to the fact that Saddam was constantly moving a lot of his assets and defenses around during the first 3-4 months we were involved in Desert Shield."

During the first few weeks of Desert Shield, all of the pieces of the great Iraqi military puzzle began to fall into place. The level of knowledge on this subject had been very limited as the United States and Britain had only been casual observers to the war between Iran and Iraq. It was common knowledge that Iraq was a military force to be reckoned with, but just how powerful they were, was something that had never registered ... until now. Satellite and U2 surveillance had come up with some alarming imagery. The entire country of Iraq was an armed camp and it contained some of the most sophisticated air defenses in the world. It appeared, for a period of time, that Saddam was correct when he stated that a war against the Coalition would be the "Mother of all Battles." It did not take the military leaders of Desert Shield long to realize that they would rely on the F-117 more than they ever imagined and that putting conventional aircraft up against the guns that ringed Baghdad would be very costly. This only left two weapons systems that would have a chance of survival: the Stealth and the Cruise missiles.

Upper management's interest in the 37th Wing spawned a few VIP trips down to Khamis. There were several high-ranking officers who were very skeptical about the F-117's chances and that they just might be more show than go. Fortunately, General Schwarzkopf's opinion was very positive and his visit was reassuring to the Stealth mission planners. He received a detailed briefing from several members of the MPC, including Majors Leatherman and Boyer. Later on in the war, the Wing had visits from General Colin Powell and Secretary of Defense Cheney and they were impressed with what was being accomplished. Basically, the 37th was left alone to handle business the way the pilots had trained and the end product was the outstanding results that they got.

The selection of targets did not originate in the White House. It was done by skilled military planners, in theatre, that got their information from up-to-date photos. These Intel types had the knowledge and expertise to recognize the vital nature of each target and they could prioritize them by how important they were to the overall military picture. From the time the first bomb was dropped, the war was run the way any war should be ... by competent military leaders. Major K.D. Boyer continues, "We had to have accurate and up-to-date imaging from the photos. This is what gave us the knowledge and ability, with our infrared targeting system, to take out the targets. We had some problems at first, in getting the pictures we needed. With the help of Colonel Whitley, we were eventually able to get what we needed and the problem never cropped up for the remainder of Shield or Storm. Right after the war began, there were some statements made to the press as to what the Coalition forces were going after early on, but Saddam Hussein made no changes in his defenses. The reason for this was probably the fact that during the seven year war with Iran, the city of Baghdad was only attacked twice. In one attack, the Iranians didn't get a single bomb within the city and all their aircraft were turned back without being effective. In the second attack the bombs were randomly lobbed into the city with no rhyme or reason and no damage done. This would have accounted for Saddam's air of confidence.

"In our planning sessions we had to consider quite a few things. We knew that the enemy had very little, if any, accurate Intelligence on the capabilities of the F-117. At the same time, we knew we were up against the fourth largest Army in the world and the sixth biggest Air Force. Iraq also had one of the most sophisticated integrated air defense systems, fully automated, reporting posts, all feeding into the central command. This kept Baghdad abreast of any activities detected by radar any where over Iraq. This information would filter down to one of those sector operations centers which could also go to an intercept operations center and then on to the Air Defense Operations Center (ADOC), just north of Baghdad. All of these sectors were targets on Night One, because we had to blind them so they could not see what we were doing and where we were going."

Dating back to the Tonopah days, mission planning was handled by a $10 million computer that was aptly named "Elvira ... Mistress of the Dark." It was a multi-ton piece of equipment that had been designed by Lockheed and it was self contained in a large trailer. When the 37th got orders to move the 415th to Saudi Arabia, the massive computer was loaded into a C-5 Galaxy and flown over to Khamis. Early on in September, it became apparent that Elvira was not going to be able to effectively handle the load that was going to be put on her. She was really designed for the original mission of the F-117, which was for covert strikes of just a few aircraft in which they had many days to plan and re-plan and work it out. It was very good at doing its job, which was planning the simpler missions. However, it just could not keep up with the number of sorties that the 37th was having to fly and the large number of assigned targets that were coming down from CENTAF. Elvira was mainly for threat avoidance, based upon the signature of the aircraft, which was very essential to the success of the mission.

During the latter part of Desert Shield, the F-117s would run their practice missions every night across Saudi Arabia and up to the Iraq border. These border runs were to constantly test the radar capabilities of the enemy and it quickly became obvious that, fully stealthed up, the F-117 was not being detected by the Iraqis. However, the tankers or any other conventional aircraft type, that was in the area, was being picked up. This fact fueled the confidence level of the black jet's pilots.

The close relationship developed among Intel people, the EWOs, and the pilots in the mission planning cell was essential to the ultimate success of the F-117 over Iraq. Major Boyer explains briefly about the scheme of things within the cell. "The EWOs have a vast knowledge of the different radars that were built into the Iraqi integrated air defense system. One of the keys to this entire mission planning is the Intelligence section. They handle all of the imagery, get all the right pictures, and at the same time, they were the hardest working bunch. They spent long hours gathering information and trying to come up with who's talking to whom, what types of radars are there, how many of them were there, and why they were in that particular location. I remember briefing the pilots on the intercept capabilities of some of the SAMs. We hone it down to where there may be two options as to what is the safest route into a target. We go over these with each pilot. Sometimes the safest route might increase the risk of col-lateral damage, civilian casualties, etc. We had strict rules about dropping bombs when we did not have our target pinpointed. We

Major Rod Shrader is greeted by other Air Force types after his long flight from Tonopah, Nevada to NAS Memphis in October 1991. This period was in the middle of the Air Shows that had the Stealth fighter in high demand by the public. Of all the military aircraft allowed at open houses, the F-117 was the biggest crowd draw. The glory and hype that was created by the F-117 during Desert Storm had not yet died down and most all of the general population were wanting to get a firsthand look at this unusual plane. Major Shrader flew numerous missions over Baghdad during the first two weeks of the Gulf War. (Warren E. Thompson)

all know about the wall of fire that the F-117s went through on Night One and it wasn't just blind luck that brought them through it. The routes were well planned out and the only thing left to chance was a random hit. We manually planned the routes out and everything was taken into consideration.

"Getting back to Elvira … . Back in September 1990, we discovered a fidelity issue and it wasn't because of constraints of the planning grid system that it was given. It was possible for a human to come up with a more accurate route that better maximized the stealthy capabilities by not being constrained to the grid planning system that Elvira used. With this in mind, from September on, all of the EWOs did their planning manually. Since that time, new computers have been created to fully exploit the stealthiness of the aircraft."

Usually the frag (list of targets) would come in about 10:00 P.M. for the next night's missions. All members of the planning team would work into the night and usually through the next day. With the heavy workload that was coming down from CENTAF to the 37th Wing, it took all night to plan so the pilots would have plenty of time to be briefed and study their target photos to the extent that they could fly the mission in their minds. One of the planners stated that there were literally thousands of missions planned but not nearly that many were actually flown. What this meant was that the EWOs flew each mission several times on the drawing board, tweaking it each time, until it was definitely the safest and most efficient route to the target.

With the countless hours that were involved in planning the missions, there was one thing that could throw everything off and that was last-minute orders coming down to change a target, better known as to "re-roll" a mission. Some of the changes were insignificant and they generated numerous phone calls to CENTAF by 37th Wing Commander Al Whitley. However, there were a few that were critical and there was no choice but to re-roll them. Once of the most urgent changes came down late one evening and it is remembered by Captain Jim Mastny. "I don't recall the exact day of the war that this mission was re-rolled but at the time the order came down, the entire planning team was present. On this particular night, we had just finished planning the first go of the evening and had just completed the briefings. I remember Colonel Klause was one of the pilots involved in the change. He had just finished briefing his mission and at that time, we were notified to change our plans and immediately attack some Soviet-made bombers that were on an airfield. There were four bombers involved and I believe two were Bisons and two were Badgers. Intelligence had determined that the bombers were loaded with chemical weapons and would be ready to take off at dawn. We had a very short time frame with which to plan this out, but we accomplished it and the mission was successful.

"We would be using Colonel Klause and one other pilot on this strike. Each would have to make two passes over the targets which would give them a total of four bombs on two aircraft. They would be required to loop around and come back over the airfield for their final bomb releases. There was no set time that we had to wait to come back over, so the time-gap selection was left up to the pilots and was based on the number of threats contained within the loop. The Iraqis were constantly looking for a time pattern from the first attack until the second was carried out. They would just fly out over a relatively safe area, make a wide loop, and come back in. We selected eleven minutes for this break. The reason we were constantly picking new and different time gaps was because the Triple-A would typically fire for a short period of time and at the end of that time, they would have to shut down to change barrels or cool the guns down. We had a time frame of "x" number of minutes that we could re-attack and feel relatively safe. If we were to have gone back, say in two minutes, we would have flown into a firestorm. I remember that both of our F-117s hit their targets and they got some big secondary explosions as a result. The bombers were probably loaded with fuel. The video tapes proved that all four had been destroyed. This was one mission where the re-roll was well worth the effort!"

Due to the fact that CENTAF Intel was getting so good, the number of newly "discovered" targets continued to grow each day. Some of them were determined to be extremely dangerous, especially anything to do with chemical weapons or the nuclear facilities. Saddam had gassed the Iranians so many times during their war that for this to happen to friendly troops along the border was considered very probable. Thus, as mentioned above, some of the re-rolled missions deserved top priority. Jerry Leatherman adds to Jim Mastny's comments. "I can remember the re-roll we did on the bombers loaded with chemical weapons. Doing this particular mission again wasn't that unusual. The way the cycle would work was pretty much like when you flew a mission one night and got back, then you would start calling Riyadh to get the frags for the following night because you would be on the planning session and not flying that next night. I remember one instance, in particular, where Marcel Kerdavid was doing a briefing and we got a call during the middle of it telling us that everything had been changed. 'Not only are you not going to target 'x,' everyone is going to another target area!' Ordinarily this would have been almost impossible (time consuming), but we got so good at working these packages that some of the changes were done in a short period of time. It was also a very good thing that we had been so effective the first few nights, in taking out key targets, because it allowed non-stealthy types to get in and inflict a considerable amount of damage on other Iraqi assets."

When the mission planning had been completed for that night's sorties, the pilots would come in for a short briefing. Each pilot had a separate assignment and worked as a lone striker with the exception of when there were two aircraft assigned to take out the same target and even then, there was no communication with each other. They had specific times and altitudes over the target, so realistically speaking, each was on his own. Major Bouley explains exactly what was done in the planning cell to prepare each pilot for that night's tasking. "The target folders that each pilot received from us included his flight plans for the mission. We would always print out a hard copy for each of them even though the plan had been put into the computer. The hard copies would come in handy if the pilot lost his computers and navigation as it once did to me and a couple of other pilots.

"You would also have target photos in the folder along with vital data on the strike routes from the EWOs, egress info, survival data, etc. The target photos were a complete package and these were all assembled at briefing. Once the session began we would hand out the target folders to the individual pilots and the briefing would begin with a time hack (everyone would synchronize their watches to the second). We would go over the objectives for the night and also 'need to know' information. The weather conditions over Iraq would also be given some attention. Since each pilot had his own assignment, we would give a quick overview about the night's targets in general. The pilots would constantly be scanning their photos, offset points, etc., while the briefing was in progress. Then we would wrap it up by the DO or one of the squadron COs saying a few words. Then there would be a question period when the pilots could ask anything they wanted about their specific targets. There would always be some mission planners hanging around during the briefing just in case some last minute changes came down from above. They were all capable of coming up with a quick fix when it was needed."

There can never be too much said about good old American ingenuity! Going all the way back to the bleak days of the Cactus Air Force on Guadalcanal, it was the ability of its military to adapt and adjust to the worst conditions that has kept this country so strong! This has remained true even through the transformation of our society from a slow-paced conventional lifestyle to a fast-paced, high-tech mode. Our military is especially motivated to stay on the cutting edge of advanced weaponry and the Stealth concept has to be at the top of the list. It took a lot of manpower and "smarts" to produce the F-117 Nighthawk. Taking the aircraft from the production line to an operational mode was just about as difficult. One of the unsung standouts during the latter phase came into the program, did his tour, and moved on. But he left a valuable "mark" on the mission planners and the pilots who were to fly the dangerous, complicated sorties over Iraq.

Captain Scott Stimpert sheds some light on what this individual contributed to the program. "As best I can remember, we were flying a 14/10/14 sortie rate for the three shifts each night. (The first wave would have 14 aircraft, the second wave would have 10 aircraft, the third wave would have 14 aircraft.) It was an extremely tough schedule to plan and execute, but there was a guy that made our job much easier and if no one has mentioned him yet, then I will. His name is Dale 'Sledge' Hanner. Dale left the program prior to the start of the Gulf War. In my estimation, he was one of the best guys that ever flew the F-117. Not only was he great in the cockpit, but he was a computer programmer in his spare time. He spent a lot of time developing a program called the 'Hanner Planner.' It was mission-planning software. We used the Hanner Planner every night in training back at Tonopah. It was worth its weight in gold to us.

"Basically, it worked this way: we had hundreds of points identified in the states, by number, that were either IPs or targets. They were all entered into a huge data base in the planner. When it came time to plan the mission, you would put the route together based on points you would be going through. Say, you take off, then you go to Point 7 then 27 then 81 and so on around from point to point. Then you would go over to the Hanner Planner and you would enter in those points. It would automatically spit out all the pertinent data you needed for the mission. After it came apparent that we were not going to be able to use Elvira the way we thought and that the mission planning needs were taxing the mission planning resources to the limit, we started using the 'Planner' in the Gulf War. We identified a bunch of points on the ground; which ones were IPs and which ones were targets. Of course, we already had those coordinates and then we started planning our routes off the Hanner Planner points and started printing up our Form-70s. Dale was long gone from the Stealth program before we ever started using his program in combat. When we were trying to do no-nonsense, rapid-fire, short-term planning, it was essential. Dale deserves credit for mission-planning software that he built on his own time and with his own money. As far as I know, he got no reimbursement and no recognition for what he did, but he was very instrumental in the way we trained and the way we ended up flying in combat!"

To those within the Stealth community, it was the precision planning in the MPC that contributed heavily to the success of the F-117 in the war. The planners complemented the skill of the pilots and the excellent technology that had been incorporated into the aircraft at Lockheed.

Captain Rob Donaldson goes over a last-minute checklist with his crew chief to make sure he has everything he needs to carry out the mission. It is nighttime at Khamis Mushait which means that the first wave of aircraft is already inbound to their targets. Donaldson was flying the second or third strike package of the night. By the time the war was a few days old, the waves of F-117s sent out against targets in Iraq were made up of a mixture of both the 415th and 416th Squadrons. (Rose Reynolds)

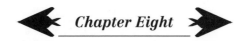
A Personal View

For as long as the United States military organizations have been around, there have been a few popular wars (with general public support). There have been numerous unpopular wars, in which dark shadows were cast all the way from the home front over to the forward airbases that were in harm's way. Recent generations were subjected to such political fiascoes as the "Police Action" in Korea and the War in Southeast Asia. The Korean War did stop the spread of communism to that country, but it was too soon after World War II for the public to become emotionally involved. There is nothing to be gained by dwelling on Vietnam except the fact that it was so unpopular that it almost split this great country in half.

The invasion of Kuwait by Iraq had produced an effect on the American public that can only be compared with the early days of World War II; back when there was right and wrong, or even more specific, good and evil. Positive public sentiment was on a slow build as Desert Shield began spooling up. A lot of this interest was generated by the Stealth itself, especially when it had been introduced to the rank and file in its debut at Nellis AFB. Going into the Crisis in the Gulf, the Americans held its military in the highest esteem it had witnessed in more than a generation.

One of the first major appearances for the F-117 took place at Oshkosh '90. This event was a close kin to the big air shows over in Europe as far as drawing huge crowds and getting national media coverage. Captain Jeff "Jammer" Moore took part in the show and recalls the excitement the black jet created, before Saddam Hussein made his ill-fated move. "It was a great pleasure for me to be able to participate in the Oshkosh show. It was

Scott 'Outlaw' Stimpert who flew the F-117 in from Tonopah to a huge welcome from the crowd. We put it on static display with ropes around it to keep the crowd from getting too close. The public was pretty saavy and asked a lot of questions that we could not answer. We had the lion's share of the attention from the crowd and were made to feel very special by the people that lined up to get a glimpse of our aircraft. On a related note, I was amused at the frequent astonishment of people who could not get their auto-focus cameras to focus for pictures of the jet. Convinced they were experiencing the "stealth" capability of the jet as their lenses tracked in and out of short- and long-range focus. Of course, they were only trying to focus on a flat, black, jet panel which offered no contrast. If I remember correctly, it was Neil McAskill who had the honors of flying the Stealth back to our base. It was an experience I will long remember and we had no idea that we would be flying this jet into combat just a few short months later."

During the Desert Shield / Desert Storm period, the number of letters being sent to the armed forces from the states numbered in the millions. There wasn't a single unit in any branch of the American military that did not have more letters than they could answer. This momentum was generated by the steadily increasing coverage from the media dealing with the fact that the public wanted to hear about it and view it on television. I can remember seeing the front page of a major Tennessee newspaper that was published during the early buildup. It showed a large convoy of 101st Airborne troops moving down the Interstate Highway through Nashville and all the overpasses were jammed with people and they all had American flags. No true American could look at that picture without becoming emotional. It had clearly developed into a "Them or Us" confrontation and there was no doubt in the minds of the American public as to who the good guys were!

The postal unit at Khamis Mushait did not escape the deluge of letters and packages that flooded into the Gulf Theatre. A majority of these were addressed to "any American soldier or airman." Many members of the 37th Wing developed lasting friendships with their "pen pals." The ages of these letter writers ranged from grade schoolers to teenagers to middle aged to grandparents. Most of the writers had no idea who would end up reading their letter of support! There were at least two significant stories that came out of this that were called to the author's attention, although I'm sure there were many more than this. One of these was related by 416th Squadron Commander, Lt. Colonel G.T. Gonyea. "The support from back home was the greatest! It made things much easier for everyone over there. I answered quite a few of the letters, but there was one, in particular, that will always be remembered. While I was at Khamis, one of the members of the media pool found out that we were from the same area and they requested an interview. I only agreed to do it if they used only my first name, so the interview was published as 'Greg, a Stealth Squadron Commander.' Well, there was a gentleman in North Dakota who read the interview. He read in it that I liked to play Country and Western music on my Sony Walkman while returning from the long missions. His name was Joseph Lepinske and he was a World War II veteran who had lost his left leg as a result of being wounded in combat while serving with the 103rd Field Artillery Unit in Europe.

"He held a microphone up to his radio and made two lengthy tapes of the music I had mentioned and he mailed it to; 'Greg, a Stealth Squadron Commander.' Even though some of my pilots warned me it might be a bomb, I opened it and here were these two tapes and a note. This gesture had a profound effect on me and I am still in touch with Mr. Lepinske. I got numerous hours of pleasure listening to that music as I cruised from the Iraqi border back to our base in Saudi Arabia!!! However, it was the letters from the school children that effected every one of us the most. All of our guys sent letters back to them and it was an emotional job because of the genuine concern that the kids back home seemed to have for our well being. With support like that from the home front, it would be difficult not to give 100% on any mission that we were assigned!"

Some of the letters and cards were signed by entire classrooms, and the pilots and other Stealth personnel tried to respond to each of them. The famous photograph of the F-117 over Lake Tahoe was used for autograph sessions, with each pilot using a special place on the picture where he signed. Below each signature was the pilot's "call sign" and Bandit number. These were mailed back to the classrooms where they were prominently displayed on their bulletin boards.

None of the individual stories that came from all the pen pals and supportive citizens would be able to top the one that is related by Major Joe Bouley of the 415th Squadron. "The letters that we got from back home were overwhelming to all of us. We had bins full of letters and cards and all of us tried to answer as many as we could. They were from all over the U.S. We had free mail so most all of them were responded to. The deluge of mail was compounded as most of the people [whom] we answered wrote back. I believe that this was the case in just about every unit that served in Desert Storm. Every one of them supported us 100%. One day I was handed a letter that was addressed to 'Any Pilot' and it was from a woman named Sara Caldwell. I wrote to her and she wrote back. At the time, I believe I had a regular correspondence going with at least 35 people. I don't mind telling you that Sara went to the top of the priority list quickly because her letters were so funny and entertaining. At the time, I was also corresponding with one family with four kids who lived on a farm in Wisconsin. They would send me cookies and then a six-pack of Sharp's non-alcoholic beer which was pretty cool!

"At the end of the war, I had accumulated quite a few small American flags that had been on missions with me. I sent one to every one of the people or families that I had been corresponding with. Sara had sent all of the flags to me. I went to our print shop and had a computer generated certificate made up that stated, 'This American flag had flown a such and such mission on a certain night, over Iraq.' I sent these out with a letter to all of my pen pals thanking them for their support and with the war being over, I would be leaving to go home. My correspondence with Sara continued and when I got back home, she flew out to Las Vegas to meet with me. After eight months of writing and six weeks of dating, we were married at the Excaliber in Vegas with the entire 415th Squadron in attendance. It was like something right out of a movie script."

One of the Stealth pilots made the comment that it wasn't the SAMs or Triple-A that worried him the most ... it was the fear of the batteries on his Sony Walkman running down before he got back to Khamis! As funny as it sounds, the music that they listened to from the Iraqi border and the F-117 base, was something that relaxed them after a dangerous, pressure-packed bomb run over a heavily defended target. Each of these pilots had a preference for a certain type of music or they had several tapes of a specific band. Jerry Leatherman stated, "I sure do remember relying on my Walkman! After we got back to our tankers at the border, we had that long two and a half hour flight back. I had my tape of Def Leppard ready to go and I looked forward to starting out with my favorite 'Pour Some Sugar on Me.' I guarantee you that the numbers that were on that track would keep you awake for that period of time.

"We traded a lot of tapes back and forth and the most essential item in your survival kit was an extra set of batteries! Of course if the tapes were too relaxing, you might dose off and wake up half way across Egypt!" Some of the cassette tapes that the guys voiced a strong liking for were such groups as: ZZ TOP, Jimmy Buffet, Lee Greenwood, Steve Winwood, Huey Lewis and the News, '38 Special, and Guns 'n Roses, etc. "Jammer" Moore stated that he played a lot of Steve Winwood's "Night Train," but in general he selected Lee Greenwood going in and Jimmy Buffet coming out. He explains his choices, "One helped me focus and get my mind right for the task at hand while the other let my mind escape for a while and kept me sane during a crazy time."

Scott "Outlaw" Stimpert had a very frustrating experience that involved his Walkman on the long flight over from the states. It will give you an idea of what a critical piece of equipment it was, as it was the only thing available that could fight the boredom. "I do remember that I had my compact disk player up on the HUD (heads-up display) of the aircraft all plugged in and ready to go. About one and a half hours into the long flight, all I could think about was getting to listen to some good music for the remainder of the flight over to the middle east. As we got into some very turbulent weather, I remember that it fell off the HUD down to the floor of the airplane, beyond my reach. So it is laying on the floor and I decide that what I am going to do is speed the aircraft up and then throw the power to idle, unloading a bit, allowing the player to float through and I could grab it. I speed it up, reach down (all this time, trying to keep tabs on the wingtip of the tanker in this bad weather) and all I succeed in doing is batting it deeper under my seat. From that position, there was just no reaching it. So, for the next 12.5 hours of the flight, I have no player and no tunes to listen to. It seems like a small thing, but I would have paid big money to have gotten it out from under my seat!"

Probably, the most popular item in Saudi Arabia was the telephone. It was the only means of direct communication with the families back in the states. Unfortunately, due to the number of personnel involved at the various bases, the time restrictions put on the length of the call made it very frustrating, especially after standing in line for a couple of hours. After all of this, there was no guarantee you would be able to reach any family due to the vast time differences. After several restrictions and the phones finally being cut off due to the interference with local traffic between bases, American Ingenuity finally set in with a few of the pilots. Scott Stimpert, relates how he and a few other pilots created a fool-proof method of letting their wives know they were thinking about them and that all was well. "It was very frustrating trying to get calls through to the states. One night Wes Cockman and I sat around thinking this problem over. We decided that in previous assignments, when guys wanted to make a call, they would go to phone booths and not make the calls from squadron ops or their rooms. We then wondered if there were any phone booths at Khamis. We drove around the base looking for one. The next time we were out in the tower, we asked the chief if there were any phone booths on base. He stated that on the wall of the bank, on the far side of Khamis (on the Saudi side), there was a clam-shell type booth that had a phone.

"We went over there one night, real late, in the dark and parked the truck in front of it. We then dialed a certain 800 number. The next voice we heard was an AT&T operator in Atlanta!! We wanted to keep this setup quiet, because if too many people found out about it, we would probably lose a good thing! We also briefed our wives about keeping their mouths shut and not to tell anyone that they had talked to us. It could have created a morale problem with other wives [who] were back in Vegas. We did, however, share this information with our flight commanders as this could be periodically used as a great tool for any of the pilots that were low in morale because they had not talked to their wives in a while. I never knew when I was going to have time to call my wife Terri. She was a nurse back home and was working various shifts at the hospital. Before I left for Saudi, I told her that if I ever called and left a number on her pager that was all sevens, she would know it was me and that I was thinking about her. We kept this system going until I got back home! It meant a lot to her! One of the bombs that I dropped over Iraq had a long line of 7s painted on it. Very significant!"

The 415th Squadron was the first of the Stealth squadrons to deploy to the Middle East during the early days of Desert Shield, so they would be the first to return to the states when the war ended. By being the first out, they became the appointed celebrities at all of the air shows that followed the war. For the remaining months of 1991, the F-117 had become a legend in the eyes of the public which turned out in the hundreds of thousands to get a glimpse. Jammer Moore continues with his recollections of the postwar circuit. "After the war, we became a traveling public relations show. It began to effect our much needed time to continue our training regimen, but when we started cutting back, we were told in no uncertain terms that the training would have to take a back seat to the public! Like the rest of our group,

The unusual lines of the F-117 are clearly shown here. This configuration combined with the absorbent skin of the aircraft make it practically impossible for an enemy radar scope to pick up any return. However, if the bomb bay doors were stuck open or any of its antennae were protruding, this could pose a problem for the aircraft. Once it hit the IP, the aircraft flew itself and the pilot concentrated on identifying and putting the crosshairs on his assigned targets. (DVIC DF-SC-99-00066)

I basically did an air show every other weekend. These were good deals, but they took us away from our families even more. I got to do Oshkosh and El Paso again. I also made Hawaii, Abbottsford, and a great show at Minot, North Dakota. The American public was great! They couldn't say "thank you" enough and they were in awe of what, in time you will discover, is pretty simple and straight-forward technology. The show circuit was the best place to become reacquainted with our real boss ... the American taxpayer."

Chapter Nine

Facts and Figures

Vital Statistics of the F-117 Nighthawk

Function: Designed as a fighter/attack aircraft
Prime Contractor: Lockheed Martin Aeronautics Company
Power Plant: 2 General Electric F404 engines
Dimensions: Wingspan   43 feet 4 inches
                       Length   65 feet 11 inches
                       Height   12 feet 5 inches
Maximum Gross Weight: 52,500 pounds
Speed: High subsonic
Range: Unlimited when using aerial refueling
Crew: One pilot
Armament: Internal weapons bay (no guns)

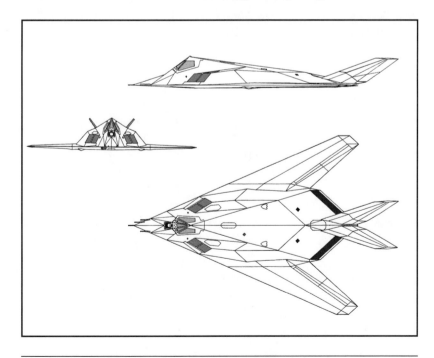

Pilots and Bandit Numbers

When each pilot was checked out in the F-117 Stealth fighter, he was given a "Bandit Number." This alone, signified that this group of pilots were members of a very select, professional, and deadly fraternity! The first USAF pilot to fly the Night Hawk was Colonel Al Whitley who was to become the Wing Commander of the Stealth during both Desert Shield and Desert Storm. After him would come a long list of pilots who would master one of the most sophisticated weapons systems ever devised by man. Today, as we move into the 21st century, the number of pilots who have checked out in the Nighthawk continues to grow. The list below of bandits and their respective numbers indicates a relatively accurate record of those pilots who were in the right place at the right time. They took the Black Jet into the "Mother of All Battles" and came out without a scratch!

Jerry Leatherman	259	Jerry Sink	294	John Savidge	322
Greg Feest	261	Joseph Salata	295	Mike Mahan	323
Jimmy Villers	262	Lee Gustin	297	Russell Travis	324
Mark Renelt	264	Dan DeCamp	298	Paul Dolson	325
Nick Santangelo	265	Neil McAskill	299	Terry Foley	327
Jim Mastny	268	Al Minnich	300	Steve Edgar	328
Don Backhus	269	Blake Bourland	301	G.T. Gonyea	329
Scott Stimpert	270	Dennis Baker	302	Wesley Wyrick	330
Frank Holmes	273	Brian Foley	303	Joe Bouley	331
Bobby Bledsoe	274	Mike Mahar	304	Lou McDonald	332
Ken Huff	275	Chuck Link	305	Clare Whitescarver	333
Don Chapman	276	Phil McDaniel	306	Steve Troyer	334
Bob Eskridge	278	Mark Lindstrom	307	Kevin Tarrant	335
Steve Marquez	279	Bob Maher	308	Rich Treadway	336
George Kelman	281	Gregg Verser	310	Ray Lynott	337
Klaus Klause	283	Miles Pound	311	Dale Zelko	338
Marcel Kerdavid	284	Rod Shrader	312	John Hesterman	339
Jerry Carpenter	285	Leo Broline	313	Steve Farnham	340
Tim Phillips	286	Barry Horne	314	Lee Archambault	341
Ralph Getchell	287	Robert Saroski	315	Steve Chappel	342
Kim Fieldstad	288	R.C. Cline	316	Mike Christensen	343
Jon Boyd	289	Dave Francis	317	Robert Huff	344
Lorin Long	290	Wes Cockman	318	Bruce Kreidler	345
Bob Warren	291	Drew Nichols	319	Don Higgins	346
Jeff Moore	292	Mike Riehl	320	John Peterson	347
Phil Mahon	293	Rob Donaldson	321	Matt Byrd	348

On 12 August 1990, special classified orders were cut to send 18 F-117s to the Middle East to join in the early buildup of air power for Desert Shield. This list shows all 22 pilots who were on the orders. Of these 22 pilots, 18 would actually fly all the way to Saudi Arabia. Four of them would act as airborne spares just in case there were any aborts en route to their final destination. This situation did not present itself, so four of the aircraft turned back around and returned to Langley AFB, eventually to make it all the way back to Tonopah. This list was, basically, made up of pilots assigned to the 415th Fighter Squadron.

Major George L. Kelman	Major Walker B. Bourland
Captain Philip A. Mahon	Major Wesley T. Wyrick
Captain Robert B. Donaldson	Captain Brian R. Foley
Captain David W. Francis	Captain Paul D. Dolson
Captain Dennis Baker	Captain Kevin C. Tarrant
Major Clarence Whitescarver	Captain Joseph A. Salata
Captain Louis N. McDonald	Captain Mark J. Lindstrom
Captain Michael D. Riehl	Major Gregory Feest
Major Daniel R. Backhus	Major Joseph R. Bouley
Captain Robert L. Warren	Captain John F. Savidge
Captain Robert Bledsoe	Lt.Colonel Gerald C. Carpenter

A very special thanks to the following individuals who contributed to the completion and accuracy of this project. Without their help this book would never have been published. I would like to think that each of them has made their mark for future generations to be able to read and understand what a small group of dedicated aviators and their support units did in the Gulf War. Their skills combined with American technology, wrote a new chapter in the book on Aerial Warfare and it is one that will never be forgotten.

Guy Aceto	Barry Horne	Mark Renelt
Luke Atwell	Ken Huff	Rose S. Reynolds
Joe Bouley	George Kelman	Mike Riehl
Jon Boyd	Marcel Kerdavid	Joseph Salata
K.D. Boyer	Jeff Lawrence	Rod Shrader
Jerry Carpenter	Jerry Leatherman	Eric Schulzinger
Jay Denney	Julie Lidie	Scott Stimpert
Rob Donaldson	Denny Lombard	William Streicher
Fred Drummond	Lorin Long	Rich Treadway
Dave Francis	Mike Mahan	Alton Whitley
Greg Gonyea	Bob Maher	Wes Wyrick
Dale Hanner	James Mastny	Dale Zelko
John Hesterman	Jeff Moore	

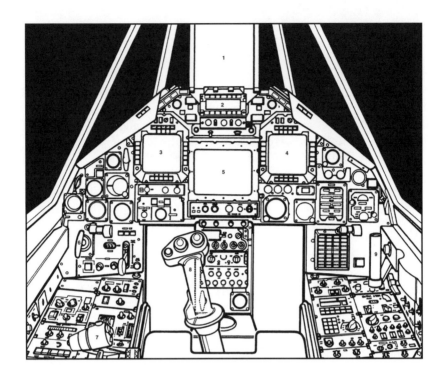

The cockpit of the F-117A is largely conventional and the following components are noted in the drawing: (1) Heads-Up Display, (2) Attack Profile and Autopilot Mode, (3) Multi-Function Display, (4) Multi-Function Display, (5) IRADS, (6) Emergency Gear Extension handle, (7) Throttle, (8) Control Stick, and (9) Canopy Locking Handle. (U.S. Air Force)

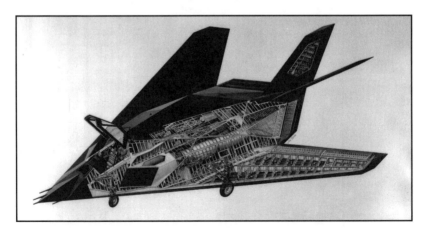

The internal structure of the F-117A. (Lockheed Martin Skunk Works)

A lot of the success of Team Stealth can be traced to the amount of time various Senior Trend and F-117 models and aircraft (shown here upside down on a pole) have spent on the RCS measurement range. At this sophisticated facility (and others) not far away from Palmdale, a great deal of testing was performed at night to minimize the chances of the aircraft being seen by uncleared personnel and passing satellites. (Lockheed Martin Skunk Works via the Dennis R. Jenkins Collection)

Acronyms and Abbreviations

ADOC	Air Defense Operations Center
AFB	Air Force Base
ATC	Air Traffic Control
AWACS	Airborne Warning and Control System
BDUs	practice bombs
C-3 targets	Command and Control Centers
CAPs	Combat Air Patrols
CENTAF	Central Command — Air Force
CENTCOM	Central Command
"com out"	all communications shut down, antennae retracted
DLIR	Downward Looking Infrared
EFs	electronic jamming aircraft
EW	Electronic Warfare
EWO	Electronic Warfare Officer
FLIR	Forward Looking Infrared
Form 70s	flight plans for each mission: route, fuel, target data, etc.
FRAG/ATO	targeting orders from CENTCOM
GBU	precision guided munitions
GCI	Ground Control Intercept
HAS	Hardened-Aircraft Shelter
HUD	Heads-up Display
INS	Inertial Navigation System
IOC	Intercept Operation Center
IP	Initial Point when starting a bomb run
IRADS	Infrared Acquisition and Designation System
low IR gradient targets	targets that do not reflect temperatures above the surrounding environment
MiG	Soviet-built fighter
MPC	Mission Planning Cell
MREs	Meals — ready-to-eat
RAM	Radar Absorbing Material
SAM	Surface-to-Air Missile
TAC	Tactical Air Command
TG	Tactical Group
TLAM	Tomahawk Land-Attack Missile
TOT	Time Over Target
Triple-A	Anti-Aircraft Artillery
USAF	United States Air Force
VTR	Video Tape Recorder